"We're so sorry Grandma, but..."

Something that won't have to be said if you prepare for long-term care—What to do before it's too late!

Don Kramer
Fraternal Insurance Counsellor

While I am a Knights of Columbus Field Agent, I have not written this book in my capacity as an agent. All of the opinions and information included in this book are my own work, not that of the Knights of Columbus.

Neither the author nor his agents, affiliates, employees or contractors shall be liable to you or any other person or entity for any loss or injury or any direct, indirect, incidental, consequential, special, punitive or similar damages, or any other damages of any nature whatsoever, arising out of any of the materials (or any portion thereof) contained or not contained in this book. By using this book, you hereby waive any and all claims against the author and his agents, affiliates, employees, and contractors arising out of your use of this book and the information contained herein.

Copyright © 2005 by Don Kramer

Published by NF Communications, Inc.

All rights reserved. No portion of this book may be reproduced mechanically, electronically, or by any other means including photocopying without written permission of the publisher.

CONTENTS

DEDICATION ix

ACKNOWLEDGEMENTS x

INTRODUCTION xv

CHAPTER ONE
HOW TO AVOID A NURSING HOME 1
Why People End up in a Nursing Home 1
Medical Crisis 2
Caregiver Burnout 6
Depleted Financial Resources 8
Gradual Deterioration of Health 8
Why Get Your Care at Home? 9

CHAPTER TWO
RETAIN YOUR PHYSICAL INDEPENDENCE AS YOU GROW OLDER 13
What Are Your Plans for When Your
 Health Changes? 13
Who Will Need Long-Term Care? 14
What About Medicaid? 16
But…There is Insurance! 17
Not All Long-Term Care Patients Are Old! 18
Maintaining Your Independence 18
Parents Need "Parenting" 20
A Crisis…A Nightmare 21
What If It Were You? 22
Caregivers Need to Adjust, Too. 23

Planning Means Choices 24

Chapter Three
Retain the Power to Choose Your Care ... 25
What Is Long-Term Care? 25
Long-Term Care Isn't… 26
Living Arrangements as You Grow Older 26
"What if?" Contingency Plans 30
Where Does Long-Term Care Start? 31
Having a Conversation About
    Long-Term Care 32
Encountering Resistance 33
Let's Put Our Cards on the Table. 34
It's All About Attitude. 35
Retain Freedom Without Burdening
    Those You Love 36
Choosing Wisely 37
Narrowing the Choices 38
The Biggest Mistake 40

Chapter Four
Plan Ahead to Stay in Your Home 43
Take Charge to Make it Happen 43
You Can Have a Better End 44
Make Financial Arrangements 45
Should Your Spouse Be Your Caregiver? 46
So What Is the Answer? 47
Put Your Wishes In Writing 48
Identify Your Allies 49
How Can You Help Yourself? 51
"We're so sorry grandma, but . . ." 53

Chapter Five
What Help Can You Expect From

Your Family? 55
When Do You Need a Caregiver? 55
Who Gives the Best Care? 56
Making It All Work 58
Caregiver Stress 58
Care for the Caregiver 59
Make the Worries Go Away 61
Safety in the Home 62
Prepare for Outside Help 64
Emotional, Psychological and Spiritual Needs 66
Joys of Giving Care 69
Beginning and Ending 70

Chapter Six
What Help Can You Expect From the Government? 75
What is Your Health Safety Net? 75
What About Medicaid? 78
The Future of Medicare and Medicaid 80
Limited Choices 81
More Choices 83

Chapter Seven
Special Issues with Dementia and Alzheimer's Disease 85
Growing Old or Alzheimer's Disease 85
Stages of Alzheimer's Disease 86
The Impact of Alzheimer's Disease on a Family 89
Stress Issues of "Long" Long-Term Care 92
Personality Changes and Cognitive Impairment 93
Don't Go It Alone 97
Keeping Your Loved One Safe 97
Care for Yourself 98

CHAPTER EIGHT
LEGAL DOCUMENTS TO CONSIDER WHEN PREPARING FOR INCAPACITY 99
Durable Power of Attorney 100
Minnesota Health Care Directive 101
Last Will and Testament 102
Trusts 103
Conservator/Guardian Nomination Form 104
Pre-Planning Your Funeral 105
Medical Assistance Planning 106

CHAPTER NINE
HOW TO PAY FOR YOUR LONG-TERM CARE ... 109
Do You Need Long-Term Care Insurance? 109
Diagram 9.1: Chances of Needing Care 110
Risk Management: Essential for
    Financial Security 113
Medicaid As An Option 114
Insurance As An Option 116
Table 9.1: Chances of Life Risk Occurences and
    Insurance Coverage for Risks 117
Immediate Annuity 119
Reverse Mortgage 120
Savings to Cover Expenses 121
What About Waiting Until Later? 122
Two Important Reasons to Get Long-Term Care
    Insurance 123
Choices and Flexibility 124
Building Economic Independence 125
Table 9.2: Who Pays for Long-Term Care? 126
What Will It Cost? 126
What's Around the Corner? 127
Unique Coverage and Benefits 128
Budgeting for Long-Term Care Insurance 129
Five Ways to Potentially Reduce the Cost of

Long-Term Care Insurance 129
Should You Buy Long-Term Care Insurance? 132

CHAPTER TEN
ALL ABOUT LONG-TERM CARE INSURANCE ... 135
It's Not Easy… 135
Don't Wait Until You Need It 137
What Exactly Will You Need? 138
Financial Health and Stability of Insurer 139
Designing the Right Policy for You 140
"Short and Fat" vs.
   "Long and Thin" Policy 141
Table 10.1: "Short and Fat" vs.
   "Long and Thin" Policy Comparison 142
Table 10.2: Comparison of 3 Year, 5 Year and
   Lifetime Policies 144
What's Next? 144
The Cost of Waiting 145
Table 10.3: The Cost of Waiting 145
If You Don't Qualify… 146
Two Types of Policies Available 147
Eligibility to Receive Benefits 150
Evaluating Coverage and Options 151
If You're Not Eligible for a Knights of Columbus
   Policy… 153
Using LifePlans Provider Pathway Program for the
   Services You Need 154
Your Knights of Columbus Long-Term Care Policy
   Does More! 156
Tax Incentives 157
Something for Everyone 158
Knights of Columbus Insurance: There
   When You Need It 159
Asking the Right Questions 160

APPENDIX 163
BIOGRAPHY 165

DEDICATION

To my brother, Father Pete Kramer, may he rest in peace after struggling with cancer for ten years and spending time in home care, assisted living, and a nursing home.

x *"We're so sorry Grandma, but..."*

ACKNOWLEDGEMENTS

Without the experiences of living with and dealing with those who have died in my family and my wife's family, this book would never have been conceived. First and foremost, I thank them for all I learned from them. The way they handled the issues of declining health made an invaluable contribution to the ideas in this book. They have been the foundation for creative inspiration.

I gratefully acknowledge Sylvia, my wife. Her support, encouragement and assistance with the book along with the many hours of care giving to her parents have been most inspiring. She has helped transform a vision of this book into reality. I am grateful to my children and grandchildren for the love, care and concern they expressed for their grandparents and great-grandparents in their time of need. They have already practiced for the day if and when I need care!

A special acknowledgement goes to Lori Skibbie for her contribution of the chapter on the legal issues surrounding long-term care. Her training and experience as an elder care attorney provided valuable insights into one of the more complex issues associated with planning for long-term care. Also to Mary Marich, my daughter, for her editing help.

Additionally, I want to thank my professional colleagues Terence Brennan, Bill Clement, Ted Kaminski, and Wes Oglesbee for their friendship and support. To Dale Robinson, my general agent who helped me get into this field and supported me in many ways. A special thanks goes to Brian Burns, Frank O'Connor, Ben Timko, and Tom Wagner for the invaluable contributions and insight they provided in reviewing portions of the manuscript. These dedicated individuals' belief in me has been most encouraging.

Foreword

In 25 years of working with families to help them avoid costly financial mistakes, there are only a few resources that I have chosen to answer the critical questions at each stage of life; Don Kramer's "We're so sorry Grandma, but..." is one of them. It is a "must read" for those seeking insights into Long-Term Care. I highly recommend it even if they don't want or can't get coverage.

This is an important book for the professional working in the field of Long-Term Care. More importantly, it is a book for people looking for answers. Don's insights into the field of Long-Term Care offer safety and security in a sea of confusion. Traps, uncertainties and regrets can be avoided by a review of this work. He backs up his work with research, logic, and experience. This excellent resource answers the key questions that my members need, to give them the feeling that they can make the right choice for their future.

Anyone considering protecting themselves with a Long-Term Care policy needs to read it. Whether my Knights of Columbus members qualify for coverage or not they will find great comfort in the very wise words of this book.

Vincent M. Polis, FICF
Knights of Columbus Field Agent
Lancaster, California, U.S.A.

"We're so sorry Grandma, but..."

INTRODUCTION

Now, more than ever, the issue of long-term care is a <u>critically important</u> component of sound financial planning. Failing to effectively plan for this significant looming expense could very well leave you—and your family—financially, physically, and emotionally devastated.

Today, people are living longer than any previous generation in history. In the United States in 1900, the average life expectancy for both sexes, all races, was only 47.3 years. By 1950, it was 68.2 years. By 2000 people reaching the age of 65 would have an average life expectancy of 82.9—<u>women living to age 84 and men to age 81</u> on average.*

In other words, if you are a man retiring at age 65, you could very well live sixteen more years after that. If you're a woman, you may live twenty years or more past your retirement date. That's why financial planning for future retirement requires a substantially new—and much more <u>long-term</u>—perspective compared with previous generations.

Does your own financial planning take into consideration the fact that you'll most likely want and need assets for ten, twenty, or even thirty years after retirement? Whether or not it does, consider the reality that the expenses of a long-term illness or injury could quickly deplete your savings and endanger your hard-earned assets.

---

* According to the National Council on the Aging, *National Vital Statistics Report, Vol. 47, No. 13, Dec. 24, 1998.*

There is no doubt you've worked hard to provide for your family—now and in the future. You've anticipated braces, college educations, and weddings. And you've planned and saved for a comfortable and well-deserved retirement. But have you planned for your long-term care needs? What are your plans to ensure that you're able to afford the health care services you'll need without having to rely on financial assistance from your children or other family members? How will you protect your financial assets—real estate, bank accounts, bonds, stocks and mutual funds, or other assets?

How important is long-term care planning? Consider that just <u>one day</u> of nursing home care costs an estimated $150—or $55,000 a year. Professional at-home health care can cost as much or more. With the skyrocketing increases in the cost of health care, it's difficult to imagine how high these numbers might go in five, ten or twenty years. Sadly, many people will not have the funds to pay for those expenses. Others could see their life savings wiped out in just a few short years—or even months.

Studies conducted by Metropolitan Life Insurance Company (MetLife) show that consumers and the media lack a basic understanding of long-term care issues. To the average person, long-term care insurance may be a completely foreign concept. In fact, many of my clients are under the <u>false</u> impression that, when the time comes, their long-term care needs will be taken care of by the government. Government programs may provide assistance only if your stay is short, and only after you have depleted your personal assets.

Long-term care costs are not covered by many health insurance plans. According to the study from

MetLife, forty-one percent of the survey participants—almost half of them—believe that long-term health care is a government entitlement that all Americans become eligible for at retirement. And they're wrong. The survey showed that only 37 percent of Americans between the ages of 40 and 70 actually have the information they need to help them make important decisions about their long-term care needs.

So how can you get educated about these issues? Let's look at the media. MetLife examined the news coverage given to long-term care issues in major media outlets—specifically, five wire services, twelve magazines, and 26 newspapers—for stories on long-term care issues. It found that, on too many occasions, the articles either <u>omitted key facts</u> or <u>presented false information</u> about long-term care. If you want to be educated, you should not rely on mainstream media for your information.

To be fair to people—and to the media—it's important to realize that **long-term care is a relatively new concept**, and therefore it's not well understood. A generation ago, people didn't expect to live much more than a few years beyond retirement. With the incredible advances in modern medical care, treatment, and diagnostic technology since then, we <u>are</u> living longer, and a longer life increases the probability that someday we will need some type of long-term care. People who think "I'll never need long-term care" should really think again.

Furthermore, as the MetLife study showed, accurate and authoritative information about the subject of long-term care, longevity, and health has <u>not</u> been readily available to the American public. For example, as I was doing research for this book in the library, the first reference to the subject of long-term care I was able to find was dated 1993. Nothing had been written or published before then! Most of the references I found were six to eight years old and a few as much as twelve years old. Fortunately, that's rapidly changing. There is now more information—although it may not be complete or accurate, as the MetLife study revealed.

My professional experience in educating clients and members of the Knights of Columbus about long-term care issues and insurance is consistent with the MetLife research. In addition, my personal experience over the years of having my mother, father-in-law, mother-in-law, and brother all needing long-term care has given me perspective and insight into long-term care issues.

This book is written primarily for the benefit of the 1.7 million members and families of the Knights of Columbus, although the concepts, facts, and ideas are useful and informative to anyone who reads it. I want to <u>educate</u> people about the issues of long-term care and the immediate need to begin financially planning for such a huge expense in the months and years to come. I want to <u>dispel</u> the inaccurate assumptions many people have, such as the one that "the government will take care of me." I will highlight problems and explore solutions so that people can make good decisions about preparing for the expenses of long-term care.

Please keep in mind that the perspectives, insights, and solutions presented in this book regarding long-term care <u>may also be appropriate</u> for your aging parents or other relatives, for you and your spouse, and perhaps for your adult children. Share this information with them and encourage them to learn more about this subject for themselves.

Finally, as you read this book, keep in mind that statistically, you're likely to live many years after you retire. The longer you live, the greater the probability that you <u>will</u> have a health condition requiring extended or long-term care, the cost of which is rising every day. It's wise to prepare for the expenses of long-term care <u>before</u> you need it—and <u>before</u> it's too expensive—and <u>before</u> it's too late.

"We're so sorry Grandma, but..."

Chapter One

How to Avoid a Nursing Home

> "You can't do anything about the length of your life, but you can do something about its width and depth."
>
> —H. L. Mencken

In an informal survey of people I have worked with, 70 percent said that, should they ever need it, they would like to get their long-term care in their own home. Since there is no certainty about how long our life will be or whether we will ever need long-term care, let's make the best of things—making it a wide and deep life in any case.

Why People End up in a Nursing Home

There are essentially four reasons why people are put in nursing homes.

1. An unexpected medical crisis occurs.
2. Family Caregivers burnout.
3. The costs deplete available resources.
4. Health deteriorates and more care is needed.

Let's look at these one by one.

Medical Crisis

The following is the real-life story of my mother-in-law. Let's call her Grandma. She was an independent woman and, at the age of 87, lived alone as a widow. She was busy with cooking, baking, quilting, and other activities at church, at home, or elsewhere with friends. She even managed her own garden.

One day she didn't answer the phone when her daughter called her. The daughter was concerned about her, but just figured that Grandma wasn't at home and things were okay. In calling her later, the daughter found that there was still no answer. She decided to go to the house to check, and ended up having to break into the house. Grandma had fallen and was dehydrated, with bruises and rug burns on her body from attempts to get up. She was confused and in and out of consciousness. The ambulance took her to the nearest hospital; after having spent probably three days on the floor and being extremely dehydrated, she was near death. After four weeks in the hospital, there was still no diagnosis, but Grandma obviously could not live alone in her own home anymore. She was heavily medicated during this time and became more confused. My wife and I drove 600 miles to where she lived; we wanted to bring her home with us so that we could care for her. My wife was willing to quit her job and devote her full-time attention to her mother and her mother's needs. My wife's family, who lived near Grandma, did not agree that she should come live with us, even though part of my wife's experience included work in a nursing home as a registered nurse. They all felt that we lived too far away.

Instead, the family decided to put Grandma in a nursing home near them, where she remained for about two months. During that time, she never left the facility at all—not to go to church or anywhere else. When family members visited her, they found problems resulting from poor care. One day, one of her daughters visited Grandma and found her in her room screaming—an unnerving situation. After speaking with the staff about her condition, the daughter was told that the family was the problem, because Grandma didn't scream unless the family visited. The staff treated her as if she were demented.

After a few phone calls, a decision was made to transfer her to a larger hospital approximately 100 miles away. Grandma was confused, disoriented, and depressed. The doctor's diagnosis was severe constipation that took seven days in the hospital to clear up. After this occurrence, the family was more open to the idea of us taking Grandma into our home even though we lived so far away. The doctors agreed, and when she was discharged, we brought her home with us.

The doctors and hospital staff eagerly worked with us to make all the decisions and arrangements for home care. Before we made the trip to get her, we had arranged to have a hospital bed, bath chair, walker, wheelchair, and everything we would need for her care in our home. My wife took a leave at work and our family began the task of taking care of her.

Grandma was totally incapacitated when she arrived at our home. She had never received any type of physical therapy while in the nursing home and so, since she was not a small person, it took two of us to help her to the bathroom. She was confined to bed and totally dependent on us for her care. One of us was always close by, and we put a baby monitor in her room so we would be able to hear her day and night. After we consulted with local doctors, a number of medications were discontinued and Grandma regained many of her mental and physical capabilities. Within two weeks, she attended church services with us, and she continued to do so as long as she was with us. With supervision, she began walking with a walker. We took her out to eat, and her appetite was pretty much back to normal. My wife cooked many of the meals her mother had taught her to cook.

After three weeks, she actually attended our daughter's wedding. She even got out of her wheelchair for a short dance. She was never left behind again. There were grandchildren and great-grandchildren visiting her regularly, which she really enjoyed and cherished. It gave her a new life of joy and hope. She loved to read and tell stories. Her memory was great. She enjoyed her quiet time with music and grandchildren reading scripture. She even went to a great-granddaughter's piano recital, which was a real hit with her because she always loved music. We discovered her great sense of humor that we never knew she had. She really enjoyed having the grandchildren pamper her.

Within a few days of having joined us, Grandma expressed her concern that she was a burden to us. She would ask, "Why are you doing this?" and repeated that question until one day I responded with, "We are doing this because we love you and I am doing it because you gave me my wife." A smile appeared on her face, and she never mentioned it again.

Then one day after her nap, she called out over the baby monitor. When my wife went to check on her, she used her left hand to lift her right arm. The arm fell down. That was the alarm to call 911. She had had a stroke. She asked that we not leave her in the hospital. She wanted to go home. It took two days to stabilize her and back home she went, oxygen, IVs and all. MRIs showed that the internal bleeding had stopped and that the swelling of her brain was affecting her speech. We were told that it was a matter of time, only days to the end of her earthly life. Progressively, she lost her speech and then consciousness. Two and a half days later, she said goodbye with her favorite Taizé chant music, "Jesus, Remember Me," playing in the background.

We had the opportunity to bring Grandma to our home and provide homecare rather than nursing care in a nursing home. It took much effort on our part, but it was well worth it. It also took a great deal of emotional and physical energy, time, and money. We also had to look out for our own physical and emotional wellbeing. It was a challenge to take care of ourselves so that we would be better able to care for and support her.

Situations like ours happen every day. It could happen to any one of us. We were richly blessed that we were able to take care of her, and we would do it at the drop of a hat for anyone again.

Caregiver Burnout

Another reason for people being put in a nursing home is caregiver burnout. Again, a real-life story. This happened when my father-in-law—let's call him Grandpa—had major health problems including diabetes, heart problems, bypass surgery, and later, breathing problems. As his breathing became more difficult, the doctors decided to perform a biopsy of his lung. This resulted in a systemic staph infection that brought him near death. The diagnosis from the biopsy was pulmonary fibrosis.

Eventually, he recovered enough so that he could be discharged from the hospital. Fortunately, his wife was in very good health and able to care for him at home with some homecare assistance and some help from the family. As I mentioned earlier, my wife had training in nursing and had worked in hospitals and in a nursing home, and so she took responsibility for looking after his medical needs. But we were living 600 miles away, and my wife—the mother of six—began driving back and forth to see him about every two weeks. She was away from home on and off about half of the time for a year. Even when she was home, she spent many hours on the phone with doctors, homecare agencies and insurance companies to help with his care and medical needs.

My wife and my mother-in-law both became exhausted. Finally it was time for a family gathering to come up with a better plan of care and support for Grandpa. It was agreed that each family member would commit to taking on some responsibility for calling or stopping in on specific days of the week. They assisted with getting groceries, picking up prescriptions, mail, banking, cleaning house, whatever was needed. This worked fine for a while, and then there was another call. One evening, Grandpa took a bath without assistance and fell in the bathtub. The fall resulted in a ruptured bowel that ended up requiring an ileostomy. When he was discharged to come home, Grandpa began to use some home health care services. Because of an auto accident, my wife could no longer play the role she had in the past. Grandpa was then diagnosed with leukemia. My mother-in-law was no longer able to take care of everything—even with the help of the rest of the family. Grandpa now required ongoing help. Everybody was doing whatever they could and getting stressed out. He needed much more care than his loving family was able to provide. Grandpa would have to go to a nursing home because of caregiver burnout.

There was not enough help available in the community to provide him with home health care. But he had also purchased Facility Only Care insurance, and so he finally agreed to go to the nursing home on a temporary basis. He went to a nursing home for which he had served on the Board of Directors for many years. Being in the nursing home, he lost the independence of being at home, and it was easy to notice a change in his vibrancy, his energy to fight. He was giving up, especially when it began to look like the temporary situation was turning into a long-term stay. Grandpa was embarrassed and humiliated that he was not able to be independent. He now had to ask for everything. He was unable to communicate with his roommate because the roommate was deaf. Grandpa had no choices regarding food, had none of his possessions, and felt no privacy. He was missing the peace, calm, dignity, privacy and comfort of his own home. When he saw that there wouldn't be any changes in the future, he gave up. He refused to eat and, within days, he died.

Depleted Financial Resources

Some people go to live in nursing homes because the cost of care at home or in an assisted living facility has used up their money—their retirement nest egg. Unlike Grandpa's situation, in which there were not enough people available to hire to take care of him at home, sometimes money for care runs out long before the care is complete. In the beginning, hiring outside help may be possible so that the caregivers can rejuvenate and continue a "normal" life. But often, as a disease progresses and the need for care increases, money to pay for adequate care is no longer available. When all of one's personal financial assets are depleted, the only option may be Medicaid—welfare. After a lifetime of being financially self-sufficient, it can be a devastating emotional blow to have to begin relying on a government "handout". But there may be no alternative, and if Medicaid is paying the bills, the patient may have to receive care in a Medicaid-approved nursing home. Medicaid will not provide the in-home care that may be desired, so there is no option but going to a nursing home to get care.

Gradual Deterioration of Health

The fourth reason it becomes necessary to go into a nursing home is a gradual and continuing deterioration of health while living in an assisted living facility.

When someone's health deteriorates so that he or she can no longer manage alone, and the need for care is greater than what the assisted living facility provides, moving to a nursing home—where sufficient care is available—may be the only option.

This happened to my brother, Father Pete Kramer, to whom I have dedicated this book. In 1994 he developed lymphoma, requiring surgery and radiation in addition to chemotherapy on numerous occasions. He continued working as a parish priest until 1999, but because his treatments for lymphoma had leached the calcium from his spine, he could no longer stand long enough to say Mass. After being on a waiting list for Emmaus House, which is an assisted living facility supported by the diocese, he was finally able to go there to live. There he had a bedroom, a small kitchen, and shared living facilities with other priests who also needed to be in an assisted living facility. After two years there, Fr. Pete's health deteriorated and his need for care grew to the point where the staff would no longer allow him to stay. He ended up going to live in a nursing home. The move to the nursing home triggered several health problems including clinical depression requiring treatment, numerous doctors' visits, hospitalizations, and so on. After three years in the nursing home interspersed with several hospital stays, he died.

Why Get Your Care at Home?

With proper planning and support systems in place, any or all of these four situations—unexpected medical crisis, caregiver burnout, depleted financial resources, and the gradual deterioration of health—could be dealt with.

Unfortunately, nursing homes can't always afford to pay what it would take to hire capable people for the jobs that are so demanding. Nursing home pay is notoriously low. Imagine yourself being paid $9 an hour with no health insurance coverage to dress, bathe, and change the diapers of your neighbor's 90-year-old parent. And yet, that's the typical nurse's aide position. The special people who embrace this type of work—who would provide excellent care to those who need it most—often can't afford to take these jobs and if they do, they can't afford to stay for very long.

A nursing home is one of the most demanding work places on earth. The level and quality of care given to patients in a nursing home are more likely determined by the availability and quality of staff to give that care, rather than by the needs of patients. To increase the staff and offer higher salaries for staff best suited to give the emotional and physical care for patients would bankrupt the nursing home. And yet without adequate staff, a patient may not be able to be moved from an uncomfortable position until the next time the assistant visits the room. Imagine a diapered patient left for hours with a soiled diaper because there's no one to take care of it. If there isn't time to work on a patient's rehabilitation, he or she may become even more impaired, which could very well lead to the patient becoming completely bedridden. I don't share this information and my personal insights with you in order to place blame on nursing home administrators, and I don't want to paint a depressing picture of the quality of care that nursing homes provide. There are very caring and dedicated people doing the best they can in many nursing homes. Sometimes they are just simply faced with impossible situations. This is a reality that has to be faced by many nursing home patients and family members every day.

In upcoming chapters, we will look at what can be done to improve the quality of your long-term care, in any setting, if and when you need it. In Chapter 4, we will take a look specifically at what plans you can make to receive long-term care in your home, if you choose to do that. Yes, there <u>are</u> things you can do—if you start now. The key is knowing what to do and doing it. The "what to do" is what you will find in the following chapters. The fact that you are reading this shows that you <u>are</u> starting now.

Chapter Two

Retain Your Physical Independence as You Grow Older

"The highest goal of human life is to die in the peace of God."

—Mother Teresa

What Are Your Plans for When Your Health Changes?

You know that as people age, their health declines. But how much have you thought about <u>your</u> future health? Let me ask you some questions.

- How would your day-to-day life change if you were to experience a decline in your health as you grow older?

- What happens if your health changes such that you can't go shopping, you can't take care of your house and you can't even dress or bathe yourself? Who would take care of you?

- What plans have you made or are you in the process of making to accommodate the health changes that you may experience as you age?

- What would happen if there were no cure for your ailment or condition? Health care would then become a matter of comfort—physical, emotional, and spiritual—rather than medical treatment.

These are tough questions. If you're like most people, you've never really given them much serious thought, let alone started making plans to address and answer them.

You probably have health insurance, and you have always assumed that it will sufficiently provide for all of your health care needs in the months and years to come. Health insurance <u>will</u>, of course, provide for many of your health care needs—for office visits to physicians and specialists and for illnesses or injuries that can be taken care of with a short-term stay in the hospital.

But what will happen if your health change is one that <u>can't</u> be easily treated and may be <u>long-lasting</u> or <u>permanent</u>? What if it's such that you need help in your daily activities for living? Will your spouse, family, or the people you live with have the physical and financial ability to take care of you? Will one of your children or some of your relatives give up their jobs and invite you to move in with them so that they can help you? Or will they move in with you to care for you? And…is that what you would <u>want</u> to happen?

Who Will Need Long-Term Care?

Right now, when you include all age groups, one out of two people is expected to need long-term care at some time in his or her life. One out of four people needing long-term care <u>today</u> spends more than $100,000.

The need for long-term care grows significantly in the years after age 65. Marilee Driscoll in her book <u>The Complete Idiots Guide to Long-Term Care Planning</u> states: "From age 65 to 74, 12.1 percent of the people need long-term care. From ages 75 to 84, 27.2 percent need long-term care. For people over age 85, 69.8 percent need long-term care." And although most people worry these days about dementia and Alzheimer's disease, clinical depression is also a very serious health problem among the elderly. In fact, the suicide rate for elderly men is the highest of any population group, including teenage boys.

Sandra Timmerman, Ed.D., Director of the Mature Market Institute, said in April 2002, "The projected average cost for one person is $61,320 per year or $153,300 for the average nursing home stay causing many families to have to spend down their assets."

I don't have to tell you that raising a family today is costly. For many of us, there's not much money left over to put toward our long-term goals such as saving for our children's college educations or for retirement. Ideally, caring for a sick parent shouldn't be part of that equation. Yet, as with so many things in life, reality is quite different. Today, many people start families in their 30s and 40s—while their parents live well into their 70s, 80s, and 90s. They're in the middle. Experts have even coined the term, "The Sandwich Generation," to describe them as they are being squeezed between their conflicting financial obligations to their children and to their aging parents needing long-term care and financial assistance.

The cost of nursing home care varies from one part of the country to another. For the purpose of this example, let's use $50,000 per year. Nursing home costs have been going up about 5 percent a year. If you are 55 years old now and the long-term care costs continue to increase at 5 percent per year, then long-term care will cost $592 a day at age 85. The cost of nursing home care in a semi-private room at that rate would be more than $200,000 a year. You would need to have $4 million invested at 5 percent to generate enough money to pay that cost.

It's clear that the average cost of nursing home care today—or five or twenty years from now—could easily force you to deplete all of your assets or to rely on your family for help. According to the Health Insurance Association of America (1999), "Most older Americans are cared for at home; family members and friends are the sole caregiver for 70 percent of elderly people."

What About Medicaid?

Many people think that the federal government's Medicaid program will take care of everything. Well, Medicaid <u>will</u> help — but only after you've used up enough of your own financial resources so that you would be eligible for public welfare. According to the U.S. Department of Health and Human Services, in 2001, Medicare covered only 14 percent of long-term care costs of Americans. Individuals needing care, and their families, pay for <u>over one-third </u>of the high cost of long-term care out of their own pockets—savings, mutual funds, and Certificates of Deposit or whatever else they could turn into cash.

Social Security, of course, was not designed to provide or pay for long-term care at all. The Social Security Act of 1935 was designed to provide retirement benefits. The Medicare Act of 1965 was designed to provide affordable healthcare for the elderly using Social Security to fund it, but it did not really increase funding. So how will the government fund long-term care, especially when the baby boomers start to need it?

But…There is Insurance!

Long-term care insurance has been available in the United States for twenty or more years, so you've probably at least heard about it. Is that a possible solution for you? Can you afford it? How much does it cost?

Just so you know, people who do not own long-term care insurance overestimate the cost of it by an average of 50 percent.[1] It may very well cost less than you think. In Chapter 9, I'll provide you with details about the costs associated with long-term care, and I'll show you some options for paying for long-term care.

Did you know that you can buy a long-term care insurance policy that you cannot outlive? Or you could choose a policy that will provide coverage for a designated number of years. Through the Knights of

---

[1] Conning and Company, *Long-Term Care Insurance, Baby Boom or Bust,* 1999, page 18.

Columbus, we will help you design your own unique policy with exactly the coverage you need and want.

In Chapter 10, I'll explain the details of the types of insurance coverage and the costs. For now, know that the cost of the insurance depends on your age at the time of purchase and how much coverage you want and for what types of care. It's like buying a car. You can get a cheap one that will get you around, but it may not last long enough or give you the options you want—or the features that you may <u>need</u> in the future.

Not All Long-Term Care Patients Are Old!

The need for long-term care usually arises from age or chronic illness, injury or disability. Approximately 60 percent of us who reach age 65 will need long-term care at some time in our lives according to a report published in 1999 by Conning and Company titled, "Long-Term Care Insurance—Baby Boom or Bust?"

But the need for long-term care is not just an issue for retirees. Many people don't realize that the need for long-term care can strike at any time and at any age. Forty percent of people receiving long-term care services are <u>working age adults, between the ages of 18 and 64.</u> Would you be prepared to pay for long-term care if you suddenly required it next week?

Maintaining Your Independence

It's entirely possible that, if one day you were to require long-term care, you might have to ask your children for help just at the time in their lives that they're ready to send their own sons or daughters off to college. It's also entirely possible, although you may not like to think about it, that there may come a time when you need help getting dressed, eating, or bathing. Or there may come a time when you have a severe cognitive impairment like Alzheimer's disease. If—when—that time comes, you'll need to receive long-term care either in your home, in a professionally-staffed nursing home, or in an assisted living facility.

If it happens that you need to receive long-term care, how would you maintain your independence and not become a financial or physical burden to others? With your statistically-longer life expectancy and the constant discoveries and advances being made every day in the field of medicine, are you going to be able to pay for long-term care when you need it—<u>and for as long as you need it</u>?

Okay, let's back up. What happens that triggers the need for long-term care? Physically slowing down and needing a bit of help now and then are normal parts of aging. Even with all of the miracle medical treatments and devices, most of us will need help when we grow older—maybe just for the last few days of our lives or maybe for many years. After all, the average life span after someone has been diagnosed with Alzheimer's disease is about nine years.

One day you may notice that you can't do the things that you used to do and are becoming dependent on friends and relatives. You may be able to stay at home safely and happily, but many seniors live in misery in their homes, unable to care for themselves. They don't have the money to hire someone to help them and don't have family living close enough to provide help or who care enough to help. None of us would like that kind of existence.

One of the things you can do, regardless of your age today, is to **plan ahead.** We tend to keep saying, "I wouldn't want to live like that" until we **are** like that. And then we say "I've changed my mind," and by then it's too late to do much. There are many ways that we would not choose to live, but life doesn't always give us what we want.

Parents Need "Parenting"

The consequences of aging may result in a role reversal. Our parents may someday need us to "parent" them, and that can cause emotional and financial stresses on us just when we are in the process of raising our own families.

How often does that happen? According to the 1997 National Caregiver Survey conducted by the National Alliance for Caregiving and AARP, nearly one-quarter of U.S. households (22.4 million) contain a family caregiver for someone 50 years old and older. Nearly two-thirds of family caregivers work full- or part-time, and over half of these caregivers report that they have had to make some sort of workplace accommodations, such as coming in late to work or leaving early, dropping back to part-time, turning down a promotion, choosing early retirement, or giving up work entirely. <u>In other words, it happens a lot—and it's going to be happening even more as the "baby boomer" generation ages.</u>

A Crisis...A Nightmare

Sometimes it is not obvious that your spouse or family member needs care and support until a crisis occurs, and then it will seem like a nightmare. You may be called to the scene and not know where anything is. You don't know whether bills, insurance and other payments have been made or not, so you start from scratch trying to figure everything out. If there is no system in place, you may be looking through boxes and boxes of old papers to find what you need. It won't only be physical care and health issues you'll have to deal with. It may be paperwork as well, with legal, financial, and insurance documents requiring a lot of your time and attention to sort out. If you don't live nearby and have to make extended trips to assist your loved one, you'll find things to be even more difficult as a long-distance caregiver.

You may become frustrated that, although you are giving your very best care and doing everything you can possibly do to help your parent, spouse, or family member, things aren't improving. In fact, the patient's health may continue to decline. At this point you may need to think seriously about whether your family member would be better off—and more capably cared for—in a long-term care facility rather than at home. Even though you rationally decide that the long-term care facility would be best, you may still feel guilty about having him or her being placed in one.

Regardless of where your loved one lives, you'll see that they need you for much more than lodging, meals, and medication. They need your love and companionship—things that are hard to give when you are constantly drained, both physically and emotionally—drained from providing the physical care and assistance needed.

What If It Were You?

Let's turn around for a moment and imagine yourself being placed in a long-term care facility. How would you feel? What would you think?

You might be conscious of being physically removed from your family, home, and your community. You might feel lost, unsure of how you will ever adjust to this new place. You may feel that you've been rejected by your family—that you've done something wrong or hurt them, you may even feel that you are being punished. You may feel a lack of control of your surroundings. Now you are on a rigid schedule. Your meals are served at the same time each day. If you want to have a late breakfast, too bad. The lights go out whether you're ready or not. If you want to enjoy a glass of wine with a meal, that's probably not allowed. You may not even have your own telephone, but if you do, your conversations certainly won't be private because most nursing homes don't offer private rooms. You may never have shared a bedroom with anyone except your spouse, but now you are—with a total stranger!

The person going into a long-term care facility may take up to six months or more to feel comfortable in the facility and to accept that it is truly their new home. Much of the adjustment is a matter of becoming acclimated to the new environment with its different sights, smells, and sounds—and yes, schedules. It is also related to the new resident developing new relationships with caregivers and roommates. These adjustments are often more difficult because your loved one may no longer be his or her "good old self." Physical, psychological, and emotional changes—the changes that have brought him or her to the facility in the first place—can cause new insecurities that may make it more difficult than ever for him or her to relate and open up to the new community and environment.

Caregivers Need to Adjust, Too

Caregiving to a spouse or loved one who needs regular assistance creates a complex phenomenon. Stress comes from several sources and hits caregivers from several directions, combining in a way to cause physical, emotional, and mental exhaustion.

Caregiving is complicated work. The caregiver must constantly find ways to solve problems that may crop up and develop new approaches to be more efficient and effective. They must constantly draw on their own knowledge, experience, and creativity, as well as patience and inner strength.

Caregiving is hard work. Typically it allows little time off, if any. The daily routines of bathing, dressing, and toileting an adult who is physically incapacitated in some manner can consume big chunks of the caregiver's time and physical energy and stamina every day.

Caregiving can be sad work. The daily signs of increasing decline and loss are particularly frustrating when we're doing everything right and still our loved one continues to fail. Sadness, worry, depression, guilt and other emotions take their toll on caregivers as much as on the people for whom they are caring.

The typical caregiver in the home is either a spouse or a daughter, usually in her 40s or 50s. The daughter usually works outside the home, and she makes significant financial sacrifices so that she can be the caregiver. She takes unpaid time off, passes up promotions, or leaves a full-time job to work part-time. In fact, all of the children and their families make sacrifices of one type or another, and their own family life suffers as well.

The emotional price of long-term caregiving is largely paid by the patient's spouse and children, and it can be a huge price, indeed! Proper planning could avoid a lot of the problems and allow time and energy to be available for emotional and spiritual support that only the family can give. Wouldn't that make it more likely that the inevitable death would be "…in the peace of God" as Mother Teresa says?

Planning Means Choices

What are your options? Planning can't take away all of the problems associated with you or your loved one needing care, but it can take away some of the biggest ones. Long-term care planning can free your elderly parents—or someday, can free you—from feeling like huge burdens. Planning offers choices you would not have otherwise. In Chapters 3 and 4, we will look more closely at some of the options and discuss how to plan for them.

Chapter Three

Retain the Power to Choose Your Care

*"Give me a fish and I eat for a day,
teach me to fish and I eat for a lifetime!"*

—Author unknown

The quote at the beginning of this chapter expresses the value and importance of each of us learning the skills and strategies we need to minimize our dependence on others.

What Is Long-Term Care?

Long-term care is the broad spectrum of medical and support services provided to anyone who has lost some or all capacity to function on their own due to chronic illness or condition, and who is expected to need such services over a prolonged period of time.

A generation ago, long-term care was given in the home, or in nursing and rest homes. Today, long-term care can consist of care in the home by family members, perhaps with assistance from voluntary or employed help, adult day healthcare, or care in an assisted living or skilled nursing facility. Care may be for short-term rehabilitative services—after a stroke, for example—or for long-term chronic care management for a degenerative disease such as Alzheimer's.

Long-Term Care Isn't...

Let's look at what long-term care isn't. Long-term care is not the same as acute medical care. Acute medical care is short-term care primarily provided by physicians, nurses, specialists and support staff, with the expectation that your immediate, specific medical problem will be resolved. The most appropriate facility to provide acute medical care is a hospital or urgent care facility.

Living Arrangements as You Grow Older

Most people know that some long-term care can be provided within the home, although many might be surprised to learn about the extent of in-home care services available these days—and that list keeps growing! Pretty much everyone has a general understanding of what a nursing home is and the range of care services it provides to residents.

A nursing home is a group facility providing medically supervised care around the clock for people who need assistance with their daily living activities like walking, eating, dressing, bathing, and toileting or who need constant supervision because of substantial memory loss or dementia. The staff of a nursing home consists of aides, certified nursing assistants, administrators, and nurses. To meet state and federal regulations, there must be easy access to a physician whenever medical care is needed, and a physician must see every resident at least once a month.

The area of greatest confusion is assisted living—an exciting and relatively new concept that offers many more options and choices because it meets some very specific long-term care needs that haven't been addressed by other types of institutions.

Assisted living facilities include board and care homes and residential care facilities. A residential care facility provides room, meals, and activities for people independently able to care for most of their own daily needs. Those who live in residential care facilities are free to come and go as they wish, setting their own schedule. Residential care facilities are not required to have physicians or nurses on staff, but they may contract with a home health care agency for on-call medical care in the resident's apartment in case of illness. The facility may also offer minimal assistance with basic activities of daily living such as dressing and bathing. These facilities are usually not licensed by the state to accommodate an individual requiring significant medical care and/or assistance with the activities of daily living.

Think of an assisted living facility essentially as a boarding house for older people—an upscale or even elegant boarding house. The growing market for assisted living facilities has provided opportunities for developers and owners to design and structure them in a variety of ways to accommodate the desires and needs of prospective residents. Assisted living is different from nursing home care, and because each state has its own regulations and definitions, there can be a blurring of lines between which is which.

However, the Assisted Living Federation of America, the American Healthcare Association, the American Association of Homes and Services of the Aging, and the National Center for Assisted Living have all endorsed some standard definitions. They include the following:

Active Adult Communities include for sale single-family homes, town houses, cluster homes, mobile homes, and condominiums, which offer no specialized health care services and are restricted to adults age 55 and older. Residents generally lead an independent lifestyle. These communities aren't equipped to provide increasing medical and physical care that their residents may ultimately need as they age and their health declines. These communities may offer numerous amenities for residents, including a clubhouse, golf course, and other recreational spaces. Outdoor maintenance is normally included in the monthly homeowner's association or condominium fee.

Senior apartments are multifamily residential rental properties restricted to adults ages 55 and older. These properties don't have central kitchen facilities and generally don't provide meals to residents, but may offer community rooms, organized social activities and other amenities.

Independent living communities are age-restricted, multi-family rental properties with central dining facilities that provide residents access to meals and services such as housekeeping, linen service, transportation, and social and recreational activities. Most of these properties do not provide residents with assistance for activities of daily living such as supervision of medication, bathing, dressing, toileting, or other kinds of personal assistance. There are no licensed skilled nursing beds on the property.

Assisted living residences are state-regulated rental properties that provide the same services as independent living communities but also provide, in the majority of units, supportive care by trained employees to residents who are unable to live independently and require regular assistance with activities of daily living including management of medication, bathing, dressing, toileting, and eating. These properties may have nursing beds, but the majority of units are licensed for assisted living only. These properties may also have special wings or floors dedicated to residents with Alzheimer's disease or other forms of dementia. A facility that specializes in caring for patients with Alzheimer's disease or other forms of dementia but is not licensed as a nursing facility is not considered to be an assisted living property. These facilities are regulated in most states, but not in all.

Nursing homes are licensed properties that are technically referred to as skilled nursing facilities or nursing facilities in which the majority of residents require 24-hour nursing or medical care. Some may include a small number of assisted living units for patients with specialized needs such as those with Alzheimer's disease. Residents may pay an all-inclusive daily fee or pay weekly or monthly rent. In most cases, these properties are licensed for Medicaid or Medicare reimbursement and are subject to federal oversight.

Continuing Care Retirement Communities (CCRCs) are age-restricted properties that provide a combination of independent living, assisted living and skilled nursing services (or independent living and skilled nursing) to its residents, and all such services are conveniently located on one site. Resident payment plans vary and include entrance fee, condo and rental properties. Most units are not licensed as skilled nursing facilities.

The above classifications make a lot of sense. They encompass enough detail to use them easily, and they help us to sort out the basic characteristics and differences offered by each. They also eliminate the 20 or so different names that have been used to describe assisted living projects.

"What if?" Contingency Plans

In his book, *Residence Options for Older or Disabled Clients*, law professor Lawrence Frolik states, "We've got to see old people as a long continuum now. If you're 65, there's a good chance you will live to 85 or even 95, and you have to say to yourself, 'I'll not get out of this without one more move.' Whatever type of living arrangement you pick at 65, you're likely to be moving again at around 80."[2]

Even if you have no hint about the possibility of your moving into senior housing some day, you're going to be a lot better off if you explore the idea and the options, and discuss some "what if?" contingency plans. If you want to be able to choose your care, you will need to know what your choices are, the pros and cons of each. Then make some plans now, so that

---

[2] Lawrence Frolik, Professor of Law at University of Pittsburgh School of Law and author of Residence Options for Older or Disabled Clients (Warren, Gorham & Lamont, 1997).

you're ready if you do ever need long-term care. This is probably a wise idea for you as well as for your parents or any elderly relatives. As people get older, many are fearful of losing control. If you make plans now and ask your parents how they would like to live and what services they might like to have some day, they will be able to stay in control of their lives later on. This may be one of the best things you can do for your parents—and for yourself.

Where Does Long-Term Care Start?

By now you surely get the idea that the term "long-term care" refers to <u>ongoing or even lifelong</u> assistance. The goal of long-term care is to help with day-to-day living activities. Some people mistakenly assume that most people receive long-term care in nursing homes. In fact, more than 75 percent of all people receiving long-term care assistance are <u>not</u> in nursing homes. Most reside in an assisted living facility or in their own homes—at least initially when they begin to need slightly more regular care and assistance. People normally don't move into a nursing home the first day that they need long-term care. Most move to a nursing home after receiving care in their own home or in an assisted living facility for some time. That's why the statistics we often see about "average length of nursing home stays" may not be much help in figuring out how long you may need long-term care in the future. It also confuses what type of care you're most likely to need, and the cost for long-term care down the road.

According to an AARP study, 78 percent of residents who moved out of assisted living facilities and into another setting did so because they had come to need more care than the assisted living facility could provide. The average length of stay in an assisted living facility is about two years. The need for more assistance and care usually triggers the transition from that type of facility to either a nursing home or back home to receive professional home health care services.

Having a Conversation About Long-Term Care

Since nearly half of us will need long-term care at some time in our lives, having a conversation about long-term care in advance will be helpful when the time comes to make more concrete decisions. This can be a difficult decision to make and is even more difficult if it needs to be done at a time of crisis. Advanced planning can alleviate much of the stress associated with that decision making. Being proactive helps everyone arrive at a mutual decision that is more likely to be the best solution. This all starts with having a conversation about the person's long-term care wishes, whether that is you, your parents, or another relative or friend. <u>Planning ahead makes the transition easier because many important decisions will already have been made</u> or at least discussed. The key advantage to planning ahead is that you will have more time to <u>financially prepare for the transition</u>. While many people pay for long-term care with their own funds, purchasing long-term care insurance is an excellent way to make sure you have the funds you need to pay for these expenses. Long-term care insurance may seem like a lousy deal, but frankly, right now it's just about the only deal. In Chapter 10 we'll look more closely at long-term care insurance and how to find the best plan for all those concerned.

When you initiate the conversation about long-term care, <u>don't be surprised</u> if the response you get is, "I don't have to worry. Medicare will take care of my needs." That's a common belief—and it's wrong. In Chapter 6 we will take a detailed look at what you can—and <u>can't</u>—expect from the government. You may be surprised and disappointed.

Encountering Resistance

Understand that it is normal to encounter resistance from a parent or loved one the first time or two that the topic of long-term care is brought up. Because the need for long-term care is a challenging, frightening, and depressing topic to discuss, some people need more time to think and reflect on it than others. In fact, you may well need to start and <u>re-start the conversation</u> several times over the course of a few weeks or months.

If you're dealing with parents or other loved ones, ask their permission to have the discussion. Getting permission from your loved ones shows your respect for their wishes, and honors them.

Choose the right time and environment. A significant life event like preparing and drafting a will or health care directive or applying for Social Security can provide the time and opportunity for the conversation. Family gatherings may become the right time and place to get loved ones to focus on their needs and wants concerning long-term care because other family members can be present as well.

Have the conversation in a comfortable place. A private setting without distractions is best. And don't be put off if your loved one is mentally impaired or has dementia. You may have to wait until he or she experiences a clear mental state, even though it is temporary. You'll need to keep it simple, choose easy-to-understand words, provide a brochure, letter or written notes that can be re-read later on, and explain the concept in several different ways. Above all, emphasize that you love and care about the person, and that's why the subject is so important to discuss right now. It can ensure happiness later on.

Remember, while you're thinking and talking about the issues of long-term care with a parent or loved one, it's never too early to consider your own needs and plan for your future as well.

Let's Put Our Cards on the Table

This business of getting older definitely has its problems, and some of them may ultimately become big problems. It would be foolish to pretend that the years have stopped passing or that the passing years aren't making any difference. But the difference they make and the effect they have on us depends a lot on our own attitude about getting older.

Since the day we were born, we have been aging, and aging means changing. By 65 or 70, we may have reached a point where we wish we could stop the clock. Some folks wish they could have stopped the clock much earlier.

Some people fear that, as they get older, they will outlive their usefulness. They will no longer be needed by their families, their jobs, or their communities. They fear that they will lose their physical and mental strength and no longer be able to do the things that they're doing now. They worry about not being able to drive or get around any more, and about becoming unable to take care of themselves and having to rely on other people.

And, finally, many of us fear that greatest unknown of all—death.

It's All About Attitude

Anyone who is determined to do the things that he or she has always dreamed about is <u>not</u> going to worry very much or very long about how growing older might affect their mind and body in the years to come. Their attitude will be one of hope, that they may continue to do whatever brings them satisfaction and joy as long as they live. They have faith in their own strength and ability to do what they want to do, and love life even when it sometimes causes them pain and heartache. They know that physical changes are unavoidable, and may also offer some new opportunities and challenges. Finally there will be time to read, study, or earn a college degree; time to focus on a daily exercise routine to build upper body strength; time to volunteer; time to teach the grandchildren a card game or take an afternoon nap.

Retain Freedom Without Burdening Those You Love

Personal independence can mean almost anything. In the health care field, personal independence is determined and measured by the physical ability, or inability, to perform the basic, necessary functions of everyday life. The following list of **Activities of Daily Living**, or ADLs, is used by the health care field to determine an individual's level of independence. Long-term care insurance providers use the Activities of Daily Living to determine an individual's eligibility for receiving payment for services covered.

1. **Bathing.** Giving oneself a sponge bath in either a tub or shower, including the task of getting into and out of the tub or shower.

2. **Continence.** Maintaining control of bowel or bladder function, or when unable to maintain control of bowel or bladder function, the ability to perform associated personal hygiene, including care for catheter or colostomy bag.

3. **Dressing.** Putting on and taking off all items of clothing as well as any necessary braces, fasteners or artificial limbs.

4. **Eating.** Feeding oneself by getting food into the body from a receptacle such as a plate, cup, or table, or by a feeding tube or intravenously.

5. **Toileting.** Getting to and from the toilet, getting on and off the toilet, and performing associated personal hygiene.

6. **Transferring.** Moving oneself into and out of bed, a chair, or a wheelchair.

At this point you may be interested to know that, according to a study, the average number of ADL disabilities among assisted living residents ranged from 1.7 to 2.8. The average number of limitations for nursing home residents, however, ranged from 4.4 to 4.9. This gives us an idea of the differences between the need for care and support provided by assisted living facilities and nursing home facilities.[3] In addition, the study showed that nursing home residents use more medical services, skilled nursing care, nutritional services, and social services than do assisted living residents. In contrast, assisted living residents are more likely to use transportation services. Both kinds of facilities in the study had Alzheimer's patients, and for their Alzheimer's patients, the cost of care in assisted living facilities was 16 percent less than it was in the nursing home facilities.

Choosing Wisely

In determining the most appropriate living arrangement for yourself, your spouse or parent, remember that you cannot change the resident to fit the residence. Look at residences that will best meet the needs of your loved one right from the start. Whether

---

[3] This was reported in the final report to the Department of Health and Human Services Office of Disability, Aging and Long-Term Care Policy and the Robert Wood Johnson Foundation Home Care Research Initiative prepared by Marc A. Cohen, Ph.D., and Jessica Miller, MS, in April 2000 entitled "The Use of Nursing Home and Assisted Living Facilities Among Privately Insured and Non-Privately Insured Disabled Elders."

it's a nursing home or an assisted living facility, talk to the administrators and tour the facility. Visit each facility that you're evaluating more than once. Arrange to visit during meal time and have lunch with some of the residents. Talk to the staff and see how they treat you. Notice how they treat the residents. Your goal is finding a residence that will provide the maximum independence in a homelike setting while providing individualized care and assistance. Choosing the appropriate residential setting can make all the difference in an individual's mental, physical, and social well being. That's why it's not a choice that should be made hastily.

Narrowing the Choices

First of all, accumulate a list of available facilities in the area. Family members can help in exploring the possibilities and visiting some of the residences. When you go for a visit, take family members along so you can have their impressions and observations as well as your own. For example, observe the physical aspects of the facility. Is it well maintained? Does it have a pleasant appearance? Is it clean and free from odors?

Observe the interactions between and among staff members and the residents. Are staff members engaged and happy? Are residents interacting with staff members and with each other? Are supervisory staff members present on the units? Are staff members and residents being treated courteously and respectfully? By observing these interactions you will gain an overall sense of the organizational culture and atmosphere.

Once the decision is made, it's important to establish a relationship—a partnership—with the nursing home staff regarding your loved one's care. Make sure that the staff understands the history, personality, and values of your parent, spouse or loved one who's going to reside there. That information communicates the elder's specialness so that the staff understands and appreciates his or life experience. This, in turn, will help establish care goals and policies that recognize the autonomy of the patient and the values of the family.

It is important to remember that an assisted living residence is meant to be a bridge between living at home and living in a nursing home. Therefore, an assisted living residence won't typically provide the level of continuous skilled nursing care found in nursing homes and hospitals. Also remember that accommodations, amenities, and options may vary greatly from one assisted living facility to the next—and costs may vary based on those differences. Remember that <u>Medicare does not cover the costs of living in an assisted living facility</u>. For most people, those costs are paid primarily from the resident's personal finances and/or from the family's own finances.

Instinctively many seniors are reluctant to give up control of their assets. Whoever holds the money holds the power to be free, to make choices, to maintain control of their lives. Therefore, figuring out how to pay for long-term care now will help you keep more assets in your name. Otherwise, your assets may be vulnerable if you need care.

Furthermore, just thinking about the idea of needing long-term care disturbs many people. It means, for them, the end of their independence. It may evoke images of despair and loneliness. But with adequate preparation and planning, it doesn't have to be that way. They can feel secure knowing that their medical needs will be met. They will feel more independent knowing that they have prepared in advance for emergencies and their long-term care. The question could easily shift from "how long will I live?" to "how well will I live?"

The Biggest Mistake

The younger you are, the more planning choices you're likely to have. For example, if you are under age 60 and you choose to use long-term care insurance as part of your plan, only about 7 percent of people under age 60 who apply for this insurance are declined. But if you wait until age 70 to apply, you may find yourself among the 25 percent or so whose applications are declined. So whatever your age is now, this is the time to start.

Some of us are afraid that we'll make the wrong decision. **The biggest mistake that one can make in long-term care planning is waiting too long and analyzing too much.** Set a deadline for two months from now or maybe do it just before your next birthday, since your closest birthday determines your insurance age and premiums change with age.

At some point most people give up or lose control of their care and their health—their independence. Who do they want to <u>give</u> that control to? Or, who will take the control from them? Not many are talking about it, but most people are forced to deal with it sooner or later. In subsequent chapters we will talk about what specific actions you can take and who you can expect help from. You will learn how to **make long-term care a definable expense rather than a blank check.**

According to the Urban Institute and the American Association of Homes and Services for the Aging, "Who Will Care For Us?—Addressing the Long-Term Care Workforce Crisis," October 2001, most people receive long-term care services in the home. It's where most of us want to be when we need to start depending on others. With proper planning, you can be ready to retain the power to choose where you get your care!

Chapter Four

Plan Ahead to Stay in Your Home

"I am not interested in the past. I am interested in the future, for that is where I expect to spend the rest of my life."

—Charles F. Kettering

If you want to stay in your own home for your long-term care, <u>you can do it by setting up a support system.</u> Once you decide what you want, take charge to make it happen. That's the only way you will obtain the long-term care you believe will be best for you or for your loved one.

Take Charge to Make it Happen

If you set up an appropriate support system, you won't let yourself be pushed into choices that you are not ready to make or that you don't like. Most health conditions that require you to have long-term care typically take years to develop; you can wait a few days or weeks before deciding on how you want your long-term care. Even an unexpected medical emergency that has a sense of urgency rarely requires an immediate decision about appropriate long-term care. However, don't wait until it's too late to do the appropriate planning and to set up a good, reliable support system to help you stay in your home to get your long-term care. Although research shows that 70 percent of Americans would <u>prefer</u> to be at home with loved ones in their final days, only about 25 percent die at home. Taking charge can make the difference.

You Can Have a Better End

Let's put it all into context. A year-long study by an organization called *Last Acts* published a report—"Means to a Better End: A Report on Dying in America Today," which evaluates the availability and use of key services. *Last Acts* comprises more than one thousand partner organizations, including the American Medical Association, the American Nurses Association, the American Hospital Association, and the American Association of Retired Persons.

The study found that six in ten Americans rated our current healthcare system as being only "fair" or lower; one fourth rated it as "poor." Only one in ten Americans gave the system a rating of "very good" or "excellent."

The study, conducted by Lake, Snell, Perry and Associates, surveyed 1,002 adults in 2002. Three-quarters of those surveyed had lost a loved one—a family member or close friend—within the past five years. Interestingly, people who had suffered these recent losses were as critical of the health care system as those surveyed who had not experienced a loss. Fifty-nine percent and 56 percent, respectively, gave ratings of only "fair" or worse. Three-quarters of those surveyed rated the healthcare system "fair" or lower for assuring that families' savings are not depleted by end-of-life care. Almost half (47 percent) gave a rating of "poor."

When asked to rate the healthcare system for its ability to provide emotional support for the dying and their families, 46 percent of the respondents said the system does only a "fair" or "poor" job. Four in ten believe the system is doing a "good," "very good," or "excellent" job in this area. Not surprisingly, those who had suffered a loss recently were again more likely to give a "poor" rating than those who had not. Another finding is that nearly half of the 1.6 million Americans living in nursing homes have persistent pain that is not noticed and not adequately treated.

Make Financial Arrangements

Your care is in your hands, until you give it away. If you don't make financial arrangements for the purpose of long-term care and if you are not independently wealthy, you will likely give away the power to make your own decisions about your care. Avoiding the issue won't make it go away. What would it be worth to know that you will <u>never</u> have to face the loss of dignity, respect, and freedom that institutionalization entails? If you want to invest in your future happiness and protect your health, your family, your financial net worth, and your peace of mind, <u>you must make financial arrangements for the purpose of long-term care.</u> Decide now who should be in charge of your finances when you lose the capacity. Determine what funds you will use to pay for your care. In Chapter 9, we will discuss sources of funds you can consider to pay for your long-term care.

Should Your Spouse Be Your Caregiver?

If they have the skills and ability, the best care would probably come from your spouse and your family. So why not rely on them? Let's take a look. A study by The Journal of the American Medical Association[4] showed that a spouse between the ages of 66 and 96 who is a caregiver, living with and caring for a sick spouse, has a <u>63 percent higher risk of mortality</u> than they would otherwise. The study also reported that the <u>caregiver is more prone to illness</u> and have <u>significantly higher levels of depression, anxiety, and poor health</u>. This doesn't mean that your spouse should not play a role in your long-term care and treatment. But why not shift at least some of the burden of being cared for by your spouse—or caring for your spouse—to professional caregivers? The mental and emotional strain of caregiving increases the risk of mortality in an elderly spouse. This is not a scare tactic, but to be blunt, it could kill your spouse too, if he or she has the sole responsibility to provide long-term care for you.

You have wonderful children, devoted and dedicated to taking care of you. But if your children are working, will they give up their jobs to take care of you? Two-thirds of the caregivers responding to a study by the National Alliance for Caregiving and the National Center for Women and Aging at Brandeis

---

[4] Richard Schulz, Ph.D., and Scott R. Beach, Ph.D., Caregiver as a Risk Factor for Mortality, Journal of the American Medical Association 282, No. 23, (December 15, 1999).

University (entitled, "The Met Life Juggling Act Study on Balancing Caregiving with Work and the Costs Involved") in 1999 reported that caregiving had a direct impact on their earnings. Depending on your children's ages, they may have to give up time with their spouse, their children and grandchildren just to care for you.

So What Is the Answer?

There are professional geriatric care managers available who specialize in assisting older people and their families with long-term care arrangements. They have training in gerontology, social work, nursing or counseling, and their job is to help you plan the care that you need. You, or a local family member designated by you, can also hire caregivers, either through an agency or directly, to provide part-time or full-time care for you or your spouse. Describing the process to do this is beyond the scope of this book, but be aware that there are resources available to assist you in doing all of that.

Family members and friends can handle one element of your care. Select someone to be <u>in charge of</u> doing your errands. This person may not be the one to do them, just have the responsibility to see that they get done properly. He or she can appoint or hire someone to shop, make doctor's appointments, take you to church, clean your house, do your laundry, cook for you and run errands when you are no longer able to do those things for yourself.

There are also community services available to seniors including homemaking services, delivery services, meals, home maintenance, home healthcare, respite care, adult day services, transportation, safety, energy assistance, as well as services that provide help with bill paying, paperwork, legal advice, and so on. Prices for these services vary, so be sure to check with several providers to compare costs. Some offer senior discounts and sliding fee scales. Just remember that **you don't have to do everything alone** whether you're preparing for your own care or helping someone else who needs it.

Be sure that you don't make so many demands on your family that they cannot express their love and spend time with you in other ways to keep you happy. If they're constantly drained, physically and emotionally, they can't do their primary—and most valuable—job of providing you with emotional and spiritual support. It may be more important and more valuable to have your loved ones read or write letters for you than to have them running all over town doing errands. As the patient being cared for, you need to feel safe, be comfortable, and spend precious time with family and friends. Family members and friends, in turn, will do whatever they can to make you feel loved and happy when you need it the most.

Put Your Wishes In Writing

Put your wishes about the level and quality of care you want in writing. There are legal documents that an elder care attorney can help you to understand and prepare. Get professional advice to deal with your unique situation. These legal documents create binding instructions and obligations and set forth legal consequences that can be enforced in case the written instructions are not followed.

You may trust your family members and your friends, but the only way to ensure that your specific wishes are known and followed is to put them in writing. If it is your desire to stay in your home, state it so they know that you want to stay in your home no matter what. Give your power of attorney to someone you trust who won't want to cut corners in keeping you comfortable. Even if you know that your spouse, children, or trustworthy friend will carry out your wishes without them being written down, there is no guarantee that the person will outlive you, or that he or she will remember all of the details of your wishes and instructions. The best advice that you can follow is to put your desires in writing as legal documents. It is never too soon to have your legal documents prepared. You can always change them any time your wishes change or your family situation changes. Chapter 8 deals with issues and the legal documents that you should prepare.

Identify Your Allies

Remember, what you are doing is planning for incapacity due to illness or old age. Setting up your support system involves identifying "allies" to support your wishes. Your care is in your hands and, once you can no longer make decisions for yourself, your care will be in the hands of your trusted allies. You need to be assertive and you will want to choose allies who are equally assertive to make sure that your wishes are carried out. For example, you may have to be very specific in stating what your caregivers should or should not do for you in the event of serious infirmity. Be sure your doctor supports you and sends you home to recuperate after hospitalization. When everyone knows what you want—what you would choose if you had the capacity to do so—then there are no family arguments and no ethical conflicts for physicians and healthcare staff members. Also, you will have relieved your loved ones of the burden of having to make very difficult decisions, because you have already made them—and you've put it clearly in writing for all to see.

The catechism of the Roman Catholic church states, *"We are obligated to accept life gratefully and preserve it for His honor...We are stewards, not owners, of the life God has entrusted to us. It is not ours to dispose of."*

Pope John Paul II, in his 1995 encyclical letter "Against the Culture of Death," reaffirms this point. He writes, "We see a tragic expression of all this in the spread of euthanasia — disguised and surreptitious, or practiced openly and even legally. As well as for reasons of a misguided pity at the sight of the patient suffering, euthanasia is sometimes justified by the utilitarian motive of avoiding costs which bring no return and which weigh heavily on society." Pope John Paul II has vigorously upheld that providing food and water, even when ingestion has to be medically assisted, is an ordinary means of preserving life.

When you have a legal document, a legally binding health care directive, then your wishes regarding end-of-life matters will be known and carried out. In matters of treatment, medically or otherwise, find a good physician who supports your decisions and who will respect and follow your instructions. If he or she cannot ethically support or agree to abide by your wishes, agree to disagree and get another physician. Remember, you are the world's foremost authority about yourself—not your spouse, your doctor, or anyone else.

How Can You Help Yourself?

Organize everything so you are ready in a sudden emergency. Have emergency contact numbers and a list of all medications and insurance information ready. Note where your legal documents are stored. Keep this in a place where it can be readily accessed, and certainly not in a safety deposit box where you can't always get to it.

The Knights of Columbus has a brochure (Form 250) entitled "Important Information for Survivors and Beneficiaries." Ask your field agent for a copy and record the information requested so that your survivors and/or legal guardians will have ready access to legal, financial, and insurance information and documents.

Lack of muscle strength often contributes to poor mobility and causes balance problems for older persons. Maintaining a good diet can have a profound and sustained beneficial effect. Staying healthy may well require using nutritional supplements. Keeping the mind active will help maintain mental and emotional health. Some of the greatest challenges to staying in your home are cognitive impairment, incontinence, and functional decline. Someone with a cognitive disorder may exhibit uncharacteristic behavior such as hitting, wandering, and the inability to keep themselves safe. When that happens, it will become more difficult to keep the loved one at home. In Chapter 7, we will deal with the special issues of dementia and Alzheimer's disease and the challenges to caregiving that they bring.

You may ask if there is anything you can do to help alleviate the problems with dementia. Actually, there is. Even small improvements in physical strength can make a significant improvement in how an older adult lives. For example, if someone suffering from memory loss falls and breaks a hip, he or she typically receives physical therapy services for a short time and then is given a walker to use while healing. As a result of the memory loss, however, these seniors don't remember to use the walker or how to use it properly. In some situations, they are confined to a wheelchair for their own safety and, as a result, stop walking altogether. However, with regular, ongoing strength and balance training, the need for the assistive device may be eliminated altogether so that their memory impairment is no longer a factor for concern. The person who is able to walk without a walker has good strength and balance, has a lower risk of falling, and is more likely to enjoy an active lifestyle. So a fitness program can be very helpful. Even a 30-minute walk would benefit the heart muscles, skeletal system, digestion, sleep, and frame of mind. It has been estimated that as many as 40 percent of nursing home admissions are related to falls. Much of the physical incapacity of our senior citizens—and the related costs—would be eliminated if seniors could avoid falling and the subsequent serious injuries and side effects that are associated with falls. Muscle weakness is not an inevitable consequence of aging; it can be avoided.

According to researchers at Yale University in the October 2004 issue of the *New England Journal of*

Medicine, "An ongoing exercise program consisting primarily of balance exercises and strength training can slow, if not prevent, the functional decline among older adults." Muscle loss, if it is not addressed, will eventually lead to difficulties in performing everyday activities such as getting in and out of a chair and walking.

Staying fit can improve reflexes and reduce the chance of falling. In some cases, modifying the home by adding stair railings or even moving to a home without stairs might be advisable. Housing options should be reviewed in order to eliminate potential problems with yard work, climbing stairs to a bedroom on the second floor, and so on. The number of choices of housing options is constantly increasing. The reward for reviewing these options is that you will be able to make better choices to fit your needs. Plan ahead to stay in your home. Don't wait. Do the planning, get all of the elements and "allies" in place, and then go on living, knowing that your long-term care is already arranged.

"We're so sorry Grandma, but . . ."

The Centers for Disease Control reports that nursing home residents are primarily women; there are on average about three elderly women for every elderly man being cared for in a nursing home. Why is that? It's really quite logical. It happens because when one member of a couple has failing health, the healthy spouse usually becomes the caregiver. Statistically, women tend to live longer than men. So in most cases, it's the husband whose health begins to fail first and the woman who becomes the caregiver, often ruining her own health in the process. If the husband goes into the nursing home, it is typically after care at home and a short time until the end of his life. After he passes away, the wife is left to live in the home by herself. By the time she needs long-term care, who will be her caregiver? Who will help her stay in her own home? Without her spouse, it typically is not practical or affordable for her to keep the house. So she ends up in a nursing home.

As you can see, when we do long-term care planning, it's essential to consider the health, age, and gender of the person for whom we're doing the planning. It is likely that the woman will need long-term care after her husband is gone. It is important to give special care and consideration in the planning process to ensure that she will have the same level and quality of care as she needs, for as long as she may need it. Then, no one will have to say "We're so sorry Grandma, but . . ."

Chapter Five

What Help Can You Expect From Your Family?

"My children, help your father and mother in their old age–for kindness to parents will not be forgotten, and against your sins it will be credited to you, like frost in sunshine your sins will melt away."

— Sirach 3:12-14

Every person—even those of limited means—deserves to live out their life in dignity and to experience a loving, faith-filled community. You may take for granted that you will remain vigorous and independent as you age. Hopefully you will. But keep in mind that, although you are in good health now, chronic or sudden illness may become a factor, particularly as you advance into your later years.

When Do You Need a Caregiver?

How do you know when the time has come for you to get help without someone telling you? First, examine your needs and create a list and a schedule for when those needs have to be met. Be sure your needs on the list are valid, and then be ready to describe the items on the list to a prospective helper—either a family member or paid help.

Examine your finances and calculate the cost of hiring caregivers from outside. Identify a funding source and method—or maybe more than one. Even if you intend to use unpaid family caregivers, this is still a valid exercise because most care recipients eventually do hire outside providers for at least some of their needs because their regular caregivers will require relief or "time off." Next, pursue one or more of the three primary sources of help providers: family caregivers, agency-employed aides, and aides whom you hire directly without using an employment agency.

Who Gives the Best Care?

Where will you get the care you need should you become unable to care for yourself in the future? Today, most long-term care is provided <u>not</u> by nursing homes, but in the home by family members and friends. Of the individuals who need assistance with activities of daily living on a day-to-day basis, 65 percent rely exclusively on family and friends for help.[5]

It's not at all surprising that so many people who need long-term care rely on their fellow family members. Usually the most compassionate, comprehensive, and dependable care available anywhere comes from family. They take immense pride in providing the best care possible to their loved ones.

Despite their pride, compassion, and commitment to provide comprehensive and dependable care, caregiving

---

[5] McCall, N., Editor Health Administration Press, Chicago, Illinois, "Who Will Pay for Long-Term Care? Insights From the Partnership Programs," 2001.

can be overwhelming. While there can be good times, there will also be hard times. Will your family have the desire to help you? Will they have the skills needed to take care of you? Will they have the time? Even if they have the desire, ability, time and proximity, will they successfully be able to balance the needs of their families with your needs?

Let's say you answered "yes" to all of these questions. In order to avoid caregiver burnout or at least reduce the possibility or slow the onset, some planning is necessary. It would be ideal if you are able to be your own manager. However, before it becomes impossible, identify someone who can take on the responsibility for planning, making decisions, and for providing ongoing monitoring of the services you need. Create a list and schedule of the activities of daily living for which you'll need assistance. Next to each activity, put an estimated amount of time that it may take. Then total the weekly and monthly hours on the list, discuss your list with your family caregivers and review each other's personal concerns regarding the services you need.

When you have done all of that, decide if you still want to go ahead with your family helping to meet some or all of your needs for care. Finally, once you come to an agreement, devise a strategy for preserving family strength and preventing family burnout.

If your family members cannot take care of all of your activities of daily living, identify the tasks and total hours to be assigned to outsiders. Decide the types and sources of providers you may need to hire, whether you use an employment agency or directly hire skilled providers. Your local library is probably a good starting place for getting information on employing caregivers. Finally, make plans to hold routine family meetings to review everything and make needed adjustments.

In all of this, you should retain as much of the responsibility for making decisions as possible. Your primary objective should be to ensure that your needs will be met, but you don't want to overburden your family or take over the lives of your loved ones who want to help you in whatever way they can.

Making It All Work

Family difficulties are typical. Very few families can come together in caregiving situations without some disagreement. Be honest about your situation. Be realistic about what you can expect in terms of the care your family will be able to provide you. Don't be afraid to get a professional to assist you. A family therapist, social worker, or geriatric care manager can work with you and your family to solve issues and help the family function as a supportive team. He or she may offer to conduct your family meeting, provide counseling, assess your needs, recommend services that would be useful, and find financial resources to pay for some of the services you'll need.

Caregiver Stress

Caregiver stress is a common result of providing the day-to-day, necessary, repetitive and intimate care your spouse or loved one must have. Common feelings associated with caregiving are guilt, embarrassment, helplessness, and anger. There may be guilt feelings for not always being there for your loved one. Embarrassment may occur because of uncharacteristic behavior in public or even in private that is caused by dementing diseases; assisting with the physical chores of personal hygiene can also be embarrassing, both to you and to the person you're caring for. Helplessness can very well occur because your loved one is deteriorating even though everything possible that can be done for them is being done. There may be anger as you become frustrated that you don't know what else to do—or anger and sadness because your loved one no longer recognizes you—and anger because you are the only one who wants or is able to help.

Signs of caregiver stress include depression, headaches and/or stomachaches, sleeping difficulties, being more easily upset, crying or getting angry more frequently, frequent illness, feeling desperation, inability to concentrate, and eating, smoking, or drinking more than usual.

Care for the Caregiver

So what can you do about caregiver stress? **Take care of <u>yourself</u>,** and remember that your health is very important both to you and to the person who is relying on you for help. If you become ill and unable to be the caregiver for a few days or weeks, who would be able to take your place as caregiver? If you're not sure who might do it, it is time to work out a plan for a substitute. It is best to stay healthy so that the question never comes up. Eat properly and exercise regularly. Exercising can be beneficial in reducing stress. If you can't get enough sleep, take naps.

Stay positive. Instead of looking at and thinking about what your loved one can no longer do, **focus on the things that they're still able to do.** Find humor, even if you have to look for it. Talk to others about what you're going through and how you're feeling. Support groups of caregivers with the same needs, feelings, and exhaustion can be extremely beneficial.

Don't be embarrassed about asking for help. Caregiving isn't an easy task and, when you realize that you are becoming overwhelmed with all the responsibilities of caregiving, **there are services that can provide respite care—taking your place for a day or weekend or week, so you can have time for yourself.** Depending on your community, there are different services available. Most cities have an elderly guide providing information on services in your area. You can also contact your local area agency on aging. Taking care of someone can be very hard emotionally. It can be particularly difficult when one doesn't feel well themselves. Taking care of someone else may "steal time" from free time or social life. Caregiving can cause enough stress to cause a decline in health.

A final note on stress among caregivers. **Taking care of a friend or relative can have profound effects on the caregiver's physical and emotional health.** It can be a significant risk factor for some people in developing depression.[6] Research also suggests that **mental and emotional strain experienced by the caregiver is an independent risk factor for mortality**, particularly among elderly spousal caregivers of people with Alzheimer's disease.[7] The physical, emotional,

---

[6] Keicolt-Glaser, J. and Glaser, R. (1999). "Chronic Stress and Mortality Among Older Adults" in the Journal of the American Medical Association, 282 (23), 2215-2219.

mental and spiritual changes you may experience as a result of the stress of caregiving are real—and they're more common than you might expect. You're not alone; other family caregivers around the world are trying to care for their loved ones, just as you are.

Make the Worries Go Away

In the face of all the sadness, worry, frustration, anxiety, depression, and guilt that can arise from caregiving, one might think it logical to reduce those feelings—and thus relieve the overall sense of strain. But some of these strains cannot be significantly reduced—by family members or by anyone else. Often illness can't be made less confusing. The physical demands can't necessarily be reduced. You cannot make the experience less sad and worrisome most of the time.

Even with all of the stress and physical exhaustion, many caregivers do manage to stay effective, optimistic, and in control of their own lives. The key lies in their ability to stay *energized*. Once the family or caregiver recognizes and accepts that not everything can be "fixed," they are more able to focus on the immediate challenges of maintaining the caregiving system of energy by maintaining and using a family support system. To maintain this energy, the family members must strive to preserve family life. They must help the caregivers maintain connections with family routines, rituals, celebrations, problem-solving activities,

---

[7] Schulz, F. & Beach, S. (1999). "Caregiving as a Risk Factor for Mortality: The Caregiver Health Effects Study." Journal of the American Medical Association, 282 (23), 2215-2219.

recreation, social, and spiritual activities. All of these things help the caregiver stay tuned with family life and with one another in a meaningful way, and to maintain energy and morale. It also helps the family maintain cohesion. Family life is special, and it is powerful, providing unique forms of support and encouragement that family members simply can't find anywhere else. If the family stays organized and connected to one another, caregivers can avoid exhaustion and burnout.

Safety in the Home

Here are some issues that relate to creating and maintaining a safe environment in the home for the family member receiving care. There may be more as the patient's illness progresses.

1. The oven or stove can be a fire hazard if your loved one is home alone and wants to cook something. It may become necessary to remove the knobs on the range to make it too difficult to turn on, or the range may be disconnected from its source of power.

2. Make sure that the smoke detectors in the home are working, that any detectors that are wired into the electrical system of your home have battery back-up, that the batteries work, and that you have a fire extinguisher available.

3. If you're dealing with someone with dementia or Alzheimer's disease, it is extremely important that you are able to bolt or lock doors with a key. This is particularly important when your loved one may wander in the middle of the night. A key left with a

trusted neighbor, in case of an emergency, is also advisable.

4. Household cleaning chemicals and medications need to be concealed. Your loved one may mistake a dangerous liquid for a drink.

5. If your loved one still persists about wanting to drive, hide the car keys for all of the vehicles that might be available to him or her. Even if he doesn't actually take a drive, he might still hide the keys or accidentally misplace them.

6. Stairs may be hazardous obstacles and if there are stairs, make sure that there are hand rails available on both sides. Remember that if you have stairs leading down to a basement be sure they have handrails, too.

7. It's a good idea to think about future living arrangements such as fixing a room for your loved one on the main floor of the house so that he or she won't need to use stairs. Try to keep your loved one on one story or floor of your home.

8. Illuminate the house in the evening by placing lights in the bathroom and hallways and possibly in the kitchen.

9. You may want to purchase nonskid bedroom slippers for your loved one to wear, particularly if you have hardwood floors.

10. There are many safety devices available that can be installed in a bathroom, such as grab bars, railings,

elevated toilets and toilet seats, detachable shower heads, and rubber bath mats and rubber-backed bath rugs to prevent slips and falls.

11. You may want to turn down the temperature on the water heater so that your loved one won't accidently be burned.

12. The neater the home and the room, the better. Try to remove any furnishings and accessories that really aren't needed or used. Having more open space for walking reduces the chance of a fall or bumping into things causing an accident; open space is necessary for your loved one using a walker or wheelchair.

13. Since you will not always be in the same room as your loved one, an electronic baby monitor works very well to be able to listen and be aware of their activities.

Think about what you would do for a young child or grandchild. Those same steps will be beneficial for your loved one, too.

Prepare for Outside Help

At some point, people must consider obtaining help from the outside. Change can be sudden and the need can arise instantly. Therefore, plans should be in place before there is an immediate or increased need for care. Prepare for the day when the family must seek help. Resistance because of privacy concerns are understandable; your loved one or other family members may say, "I don't want strangers in my house." It may, however, be the only choice that will effectively meet the need. By identifying appropriate resources early on, family members will be able to obtain the right kind of help at the most appropriate time. Families who wait too long or reject outside help are less able to maintain an organized, energized care system.

For some families, the increased need of care for their loved one may necessitate putting the loved one in a long-term care facility. All of the support issues that we've discussed regarding what you can expect from the family can pretty much be applied to your loved one living in a facility. There are, however, some additional things to be said about relating to your loved one once they enter an assisted living facility or nursing home.

It's critical to remember to keep all of your family members informed on developments. Relatives who live out of town and who only hear of major decisions may think that their loved one is going from one disaster to the next. Keep communication flowing with telephone calls and personal contact. Discussing the available options and reviewing possible future scenarios can be of considerable help in making important decisions that will ultimately need to be made. Those family discussions should be open to any and all ideas without being critical or negative. If everyone feels free to express opinions and suggestions without fear, more progress will be made. It's best to strive for consensus, but don't force it. If there is no agreement, try to agree on temporary or trial measures and reasonable time tables.

Obviously, finances are an important factor in deciding what type of long-term care can be provided for a spouse, parent or loved one. Caring for a person at home can be less expensive than placement in a care facility. But there are other considerations as well that may result in the decision to place your loved one in a nursing home or other facility. The frail, elderly patient with complicated medical conditions may need advanced care that is well beyond the ability of the family to provide, no matter how loving and dedicated they are. With dual wage earners and more single-parent households, many adult children—even with the best of intentions—have little time to be competent caregivers. In some families, there may not be a commitment to provide or assist with care because family bonds have been weakened by divorce and remarriage. Our mobile society separates us so that physical proximity to one another becomes an issue as to who among family members can and cannot provide care. Even when available, family caregivers can burnout.

Emotional, Psychological and Spiritual Needs

When the physical care of your loved one is relegated to a facility, he or she still has emotional, psychological and spiritual needs that can best be met by family and close friends. Regular visits are very important. Treat the resident as normally as possible. Doing things that you used to do together helps them feel more comfortable. Taking them out to lunch may be just what they need. Don't fear reminiscing. Gerontologists are showing that such a "life review" is an important adjustment mechanism that helps the elderly put their situation into perspective and deal with lingering conflicts.

Don't be afraid to seek the same amount of advice and comfort from them as you did before they moved into the nursing home. You need not take the advice, of course, but your loved one will feel a renewed sense of still being needed. Sometimes you'll have to deal with anger and frustration. Remember, sometimes you don't have to remedy the problem to provide help; just listen.

Grandparenting is an opportunity to satisfy a natural wish to continue in a family role. This allows passing on information, history, feelings, values, and attitudes to the next generation. Encourage physical intimacy between children and elderly family members with eye contact, handholding, and hugging. Encourage older children to hear their "living history" in which the older family member brings to life the history by telling the children their unique role in life. Giving adolescents a small tape recorder and plenty of tapes will start them on an oral history of the family. And remember, few things brighten your loved one's day more than receiving mail. You don't have to send a long letter; a sentimental, spiritual, cheerful or silly greeting card or postcard will be just as welcome.

If your family member complains about something, don't ever hastily dismiss that complaint. Ignoring complaints may only further damage the morale of your loved one. In most cases, all the complainant wants is for you to listen. Really try to listen to what they're saying and don't prejudge the validity of the complaint. And remember my story about Grandma whose serious medical problem was ignored even though she screamed when family members visited her. All complaints must be recognized. How one responds must be determined by the legitimacy of the complaint.

Keep in mind that when someone goes to live in a nursing home, the staff can't fully offer the same social and psychological support as friends and family, although staff members try their best to do so. That's why it's important to have contact and visit those residents. When your loved one moves into an assisted living facility or nursing home, it's helpful to try to make it their own home by bringing in some of their personal items. Decorating the room according to their wishes—photographs, a few favorite knick-knacks, a cherished rocking chair if space permits—can be very comforting.

There may come a time when you think visiting your loved one is pointless. Visiting is <u>never</u> pointless. Even if the resident is comatose, you should continue visiting. We know that hearing is one of the last senses to disappear, and no one knows exactly what a comatose person may still sense. Even if they are comatose when you visit, announce yourself with your name and then sit by the bedside and hold their hand, stroke their forehead, or whatever is comfortable for you. You can talk quietly, and the resident may hear exactly what you're saying. Another reason for regular visits is to be sure your loved one is being well cared for, and to show the staff that their patient hasn't been forgotten or neglected by their family. Staff members typically respond by giving your loved one better care because they know you will be visiting often.

Joys of Giving Care

In Chapter 1, I shared the story about providing care for my mother-in-law in our home. Our family learned a lot through that experience. Sure, we experienced the negative effects, but on the other hand, providing care in our home was also a very positive and beneficial experience for all of us. It gave us a new purpose in our family. It strengthened our interfamily relationships and gave us the opportunity to give back to the person who gave a wife and mother to us. One of the greatest sources of joy was to see the tremendous improvement after my mother-in-law came to live with us—functionally, mentally, and spiritually. She began to feel less helpless and recognized how her presence was adding value to our lives. We had the joy of her company and the peace of mind that we were making her as comfortable as possible. We were richly blessed by her presence and wish that we could have done the same for my father-in-law and my brother. We had offered to bring my father-in-law to our home as well, but he didn't want to leave his home and all the people so dear to him there. As for my brother, he too had family, friends and former parishioners that he didn't want to leave. He also stated that he didn't want to leave his doctors. We were just too far away from what was most familiar to him.

Providing round-the-clock care for someone takes a great deal of emotional and physical energy, time, and patience. We found out that as caregivers we needed to look out for our own physical and emotional well-being. We learned that taking naps can be done without feeling guilty. To care for ourselves was challenging but important. That's where family makeup is vital.

We were able to find family members to help out, giving us respite so that we could have time for ourselves once in a while. Without this family support, some of the joy we experienced would have been missed. Then we might have focused on the drudgery and become distressed.

Beginning and Ending

Since long-term care most often ends in death, some reflections on death are appropriate here. As hard as it is to deal with death's finality and certainty, it is a great help in gaining the right perspectives on that which is important and that which is not important. Are we all able to concentrate on the last reality that awaits us? Are we aware of what it means to die? Which day is greater—the one of birth or the one of death? Those last days with my mother-in-law were almost like a celebration when death had priority over everyday life. All family members were fully aware that the end of the earthly journey was near. This awareness created a relaxed atmosphere and let happiness seep in. Edward S. Gleason, *In Dying, We Live* states: "Death happens despite what we do to avoid it. Everything that begins, ends. The fact may not be welcome, but it is realistic. Death is a central part of life and despite everything it takes from us, so too it enriches and strengthens."

After the death of her father and mother, my wife Sylvia put some of her thoughts into words, and I would like to share them with you. She wrote:

"Death was not something we learned much about or discussed in my four years as a nursing student. Unfortunately, it was something we always tried to

avoid. Looking back, I see so many learning opportunities I missed because I wasn't open to death, even though patients would know, and tell me, that they would die that day—and they did.

Finally, with mom it became real to me that this moment could enrich us and strengthen us. To lie to the dying about their true condition up until the last moment is inhumane and only makes everyone poorer.

The spiritual dimension of dying was not a strength learned in school either. It seems that for the most part, the emphasis on spiritual or religious factors were dealt with after death (i.e., funeral arrangements, etc.). This was an area considered private. The focus on dying was definitely different with my mother. I gained new insight into the value of being open to sharing this intimate part of our life and how it is really caring for and empowering the dying person. It is these moments that really enrich and strengthen those of us near them. I pray that this was passed on to other family members. To learn that it is through the relationship we have with one another that we can glimpse the love of our God and Creator. This leaves us with an awesome, peaceful closure."

My wife loves the quote from Sister Dolores in the book *Mother Teresa, A Simple Path.* Sister Dolores worked as a Missionary of Charity sister with Mother Teresa. She put it this way. *"When I'm with a person in his last moments and everything is peaceful as he leaves this world, I'm reminded that we all have to go through this at some point. I have a great longing to be able to go peacefully in this beautiful way, myself. We are all meant to return to God—we come from Him and we go back to Him—so by assisting others in their final moments, we ourselves are being helped."*

Let me now share more of my journey in the care and dying of my mother-in-law. Here was a woman who, because of religious differences, did not attend our wedding nor did my father-in-law or any of their children. When we first went to visit Sylvia's family after we were married, her mother did not speak to her all week. That was how she expressed her displeasure because Sylvia married me.

But a lot happened over the years, and when it came time for her long-term care in our home, she was very much a different person, and I guess I was, too. She had never treated me with disrespect at any time and had turned into a wonderful mother-in-law. She felt so bad that we gave her our time and energy to take care of her and that she could not repay us in any way. She seemed to feel like such a bother to us and our family. Well, you know the rest from Chapter 1.

The spiritual side of life was a deep part of her. When she was in the nursing home, or for that matter when her husband was in the nursing home, there was no exchange on the spiritual part of life. All the emphasis was on the medical and the physical issues. The spiritual and emotional aspects just never seemed to fit in or get much attention. If you ever have the opportunity to be with someone over their final days in the comfort of your home or anywhere, it is a very rewarding experience if you take time. We prayed together. We laughed together, and we enjoyed each other. It truly turned her from a frustrated, helpless, dependent woman into one who realized that she was truly loved in a way that she hadn't had a chance to experience from us ever before.

Long-term care isn't just about the physical, the medical, the daily repetitive grind of care. It is about the purpose of life. Whatever you do for yourself or for your loved ones, it is something that can take you to the true meaning of life. And how you take care of it, how you fund it so you can be cared for properly, how you deal with it will make all the difference to you and to those you love.

What help can you expect from _your_ family? Do they know _your_ expectations?

Chapter Six

What Help Can You Expect From the Government?

> "The government that is big enough to give you everything you want, is big enough to take everything you've got."
>
> — **Anonymous**

Medicare, the government program for citizens 65 and older, may cover the first 20 days of skilled care in a nursing facility and may partially pay for the next 80 days with the total benefit not to exceed 100 days, as long as the person qualifies. Another way long-term care might be financed is with Medicaid—a government welfare program for those individuals living at poverty level without the ability to pay for care themselves.

What is Your Health Safety Net?

Most people know that Medicare says in matters of long-term care: "We are not paying." And neither will your health insurance. Our health care system is arranged to pay for <u>acute</u> care—and by that I mean the kind of illness or injury in which you get sick, spend a few days in the hospital, get treatment, and then go home with some new medication.

But many of our illnesses are <u>chronic</u>, meaning that they are persistent over long periods of time and may be incurable. They are illnesses such as:

- Chronic arthritis
- Parkinson's disease
- Alzheimer's disease
- Effects of stroke
- Effects of osteoporosis
- Multiple sclerosis
- Lou Gehrig's disease (ALS)
- Cancer

The biggest costs of these illnesses is not the few days individuals may spend in the hospital; it is the cost of care when they go home. Who will shop, clean, drive their car and take care of the routine activities of daily living if they can't walk? Medicare won't and neither will their health insurance. Some people think that Medicare will pay for long-term care. <u>Here are the facts about when Medicare **will** pay for long-term care:</u>

- After a person has been a hospital patient for at least three consecutives days not counting the day of discharge.
- A person is admitted to the skilled nursing facility within 30 days of his/her hospital discharge.
- The services he/she requires are related to the condition for which he/she was treated in the hospital.
- They require skilled nursing services or rehabilitation services on a daily basis. (These services, as a practical matter, can only be provided on an in-patient basis.)

- His/her doctor orders and certifies at time of admission that he/she needs skilled care services on a daily basis, and again, certifies his/her need 14 days after admission and every 30 days thereafter.
- A Utilization Review Committee of professionals regularly reviews and approves their continued need for skilled care services.
- Their stay in the skilled nursing facility is 100 days or less.

There are three levels of nursing care: convalescent, intermediate, and skilled. Only the sickest patients needing constant medical attention qualify for skilled care. It's the only kind of care that Medicare will subsidize for you. If you qualify for skilled care, Medicare pays for the first 20 days of skilled care. For days 21 to 100, it pays up to $105 per day. <u>Medicare pays nothing for treatment lasting longer than 100 days</u>.

Medicare doesn't pay for the care of Alzheimer's disease. *Modern Maturity Magazine* from AARP reported in an article that there are 4 million people in the United States who have Alzheimer's. In fact, about half of the people over age 85 in the U.S. are afflicted. Medicare Part B pays for their medications, but it won't pay for care because Medicare considers Alzheimer's an untreatable illness. There are many people who have illnesses that Medicare considers not treatable. As a result, Medicare doesn't get involved and it doesn't pay.

That's a shock to a lot of people who believe Medicare is their health safety net. The result is that we have millions of people who are tied to their residences and have to take care of their sick spouses or pay for homecare or nursing home services.

Medicare pays only 14 percent of long-term care services.[8] "Families are often shocked to discover that Medicare doesn't pay most nursing home bills. It covers only brief, acute illness requiring skilled nursing or rehabilitation, and won't pay for the kind of custodial care that most people need."[9]

What About Medicaid?

Medicaid is a joint federal/state program to provide health services to low-income people. "In all, Medicaid covers half of all the nursing home costs nationwide. But people have to spend their own assets until they qualify for the program."[10] Medicaid is administered by state agencies, and it is based on financial need and the medical necessity for the patient to receive nursing facility care. States operate under broad federal guidelines. Reimbursement rates per day for care are also set by the states. Eligibility depends on a state-determined poverty level. Although benefits last indefinitely, the state reviews all residents receiving Medicaid periodically to make sure they continue to qualify both financially and medically. In general, to be eligible for Medicaid you may keep only the house in which your spouse or dependent resides, the furniture, a car, a burial plot and funeral funds, and a small amount of cash determined by the state—sometimes as low as

---

[8] Department of Health and Human Services, HCFA, Office of the Actuary, National Health Statistics Group, Personal Healthcare Expenditures, 2001.
[9] The Wall Street Journal, March 31, 1999.
[10] CNN Financial Network, August 26, 1999.

$2,000. Generally, Medicaid does not pay for assisted living.

In order to qualify for Medicaid funding of long-term care in a nursing facility, the applicant must meet poverty requirements established by the state which take into account assets as well as income. For specific information for your state, use the information provided by the Centers for Medicare and Medicaid Services at: www.cms.hhs.gov/medicaid/allStateContacts.asp. It provides contact information for every state's Medicaid Office.

Federal regulations require a look-back period of 3 years from the date the senior applies for Medicaid and is institutionalized. Transfer of money and property is considered during the review. The look-back tries to discover whether assets were transferred out of the estate in order to qualify for coverage. In the case of certain trusts, the look-back period is five years. Once eligibility is established, Medicaid will pay for care in a nursing facility and for intermediate care facility for the mentally retarded. Other services may be available in certain states. Assets that count against the Medicaid limits include stocks, bonds, mutual funds, bank accounts, certificates of deposit, vacation homes or second homes, 401(k)s, IRAs, other qualified plans, assets held in any revocable trusts, annuities which are in the form of a lump sum, and almost everything else that you could think of that wasn't mentioned earlier in stating how you qualify for Medicaid. As much good as Medicare and Medicaid have accomplished, they have also fostered a mentality of entitlement. It was quickly seen by many families as a source to pay for long-term care. Instead of the able-bodied caring for the old and infirm, they began to rely on the government.

The Future of Medicare and Medicaid

Today many Americans are looking forward to the day when Medicare and Medicaid will be enhanced through a new government plan so that they won't have to bankrupt themselves to pay for long-term care. In the opinion of experts, it's not going to happen. Let's look at some of the reasons. Legislation has been proposed to increase the look-back period in order to qualify for Medicaid. Both houses of Congress have introduced legislation that allows an above-the-line tax deduction for long-term care insurance premiums and includes support for caregivers. This looks like a signal that the federal government wants people to take responsibility for their own long-term care and then be given some tax credit for doing it. "Through a series of actions, the federal government is also signaling its desire that individuals accept greater personal responsibility for planning and paying for their long-term care needs. Such actions include tax clarification of long-term care insurance contracts, a plan to implement a federal employees long-term care insurance plan, and expenditures on education related to the risks and costs of long-term care."[11] Legislators have been struggling for years to keep Medicare, Social Security, and Medicaid funded. It is clear that they're looking for us to fund our own long-term care. In Chapter 9, we will take a look at how long-term care can be funded and some alternative ways to pay for it. For those who are

---

[11] "The Use of Nursing Home and Assisted Living Facilities Among Privately Insured and Non-Privately Insured Disabled Elders, the Final Report to the Department of Health and Human Services Office of Disability, Aging, and Long-Term Care Policy, and the Robert Wood Johnson Foundation Homecare Research Initiative" prepared by Marc A. Cohen, Ph.D., Jessica Miller, MS.

poor and who cannot afford private insurance or don't have the means to fund long-term care for themselves, Medicaid will remain their last resort.

Limited Choices

Maybe you're thinking that there's no way that you want to pay for your own long-term care. You have worked hard all your life. You've paid your taxes. You've contributed to the community, and now it's time to collect. Well, yes, anyone can qualify for Medicaid. The question is: why would you want to?

Some people think that Medicaid recipients get worse treatment in nursing homes than private-pay residents. Others think that you'll get worse food than private-pay patients. But none of that is true. Most of the workers in a nursing home have no idea which occupants are Medicaid-funded or pay for their care privately. In fact, some states—including Minnesota—have a law that says <u>private-pay patients cannot be charged any more than Medicaid patients.</u> This is required even if the institution is losing money on those patients. For example, in one nursing home in Minnesota, Medicaid patients cause a loss of $28 per day per resident. Since private-pay residents pay the same daily rate for their care, they are also causing a $28 per person per day deficit for this nursing home. Yes, Minnesota state law requires nursing homes to charge both private-pay and Medicaid residents the same rate for the same services.

Wherever it is you get your care, if it isn't satisfactory and you are paying the bill, you can go somewhere else. If your care is being funded through

Medicaid funds, <u>you will have no choice</u>. Only with rare exceptions will Medicaid pay for a private room. But if you're paying the bill, you can choose to have a private room. You won't have to share a room with an unfamiliar resident. You might even get more than a narrow closet for storage space. <u>All in all, your choices will definitely be enhanced if you pay the fare.</u> You can also pay for other services that are not required for Medicaid patients and thereby enhance your care.

If you're counting on using Medicaid someday and will be spending down or transferring your assets so that you'll qualify, keep in mind that the rules may change before you actually need to apply for Medicaid, and you may not be eligible after all. If you look at the trend of changes Congress has made in eligibility requirements for Medicaid, you'll see that they're tightening up existing rules and broadening penalties. The look-back period has been increased from two and one-half years to three years for the transfer of assets. Certain transfers and purchases that used to be allowable are not allowed anymore.

Remember, too, that Medicaid is a public assistance program and <u>that the benefits and availability will depend on the current political climate.</u> If, even after all of these potential problems, you are still thinking about transferring assets or spending down your nest egg in order to be eligible for Medicaid, be sure you speak to an attorney with experience in elder-care and public aid law to make sure that you're not left short of assets.

If your health is compromised and you can't purchase long-term care insurance, and your finances just can't pay for it, Medicaid is your answer. If you have low income and assets and can't afford to pay for long-term care yourself, your only choice may be to apply for Medicaid for your long-term care.

More Choices

You will always have more options if you can private-pay for your care. Many elder care law attorneys are now recommending long-term care insurance as the preferred method to fund your own care. It's my hope that people who have the ability to pay for their care either out of pocket or by purchasing long-term care insurance would do so. I saw how the government supported system is stressed while serving in the Minnesota State Senate. I just don't believe the Medicare system will be able to support as many people as would like to be supported when they're ready to collect. If we all do our part, we will reduce the burden on all taxpayers and make money available for long-term care for those who absolutely cannot afford it. And yes, my wife and I do have long-term care insurance.

Chapter Seven

Special Issues with Dementia and Alzheimer's Disease

> "Methinks I should know you, and know this man;
> Yet I am doubtful: For I am mainly ignorant
> What place this is; and all the skill I have
> Remembers not these garments; nor I know not
> Where I did lodge last night."
>
> — William Shakespeare in King Lear

Just as King Lear sensed his mental decline, people for centuries have been dealing with memory loss and senility. They were considered part of the normal aging process. Forgetting names and familiar faces, confusing dates and addresses are just part of what seemed to be "growing old."

Growing Old or Alzheimer's Disease

Science has shown us that growing old is far too simple an explanation for these events that are now known to be associated with Alzheimer's disease. Science has shown us that forgetfulness in the elderly often stems from physical causes that can be treated and sometimes slowed. Sometimes, however, the cause of this confusion and forgetfulness is part of the progressive decline of Alzheimer's disease, which is an irreversible brain disorder that affects an estimated four million Americans, most of them over age 65. The Alzheimer's Association has estimated that 10 percent of people over 65 years of age and nearly half of those over 85 have Alzheimer's or some other form of dementia. Age seems to be the biggest factor for Alzheimer's, with about 3 percent of seniors age 65 to 74 having the disease, 19 percent of those age 75 to 84 and 40 percent of those ages 85 and older. It is estimated that, by 2050, the number of people with Alzheimer's is expected to reach about 14 million.

Stages of Alzheimer's Disease

In trying to understand the disease and its progression, people have begun to characterize it as occurring in stages. Typically, those who characterize it use either three or seven stages in the progression through Alzheimer's. In the three-stage characterization, they typically start with the early stage or mild stage. In the second, they call it the middle or moderate stage, and in the third, the late, severe, terminal, or end stage. Those who break the progression down into seven stages, however, give us more information about the gradual progression of the disease.

The Alzheimer's Association[12] characterizes the disease in seven stages.

Stage 1. No cognitive impairment. No apparent memory problems that are noticed by the lay person nor by the healthcare professionals.

---

12 Alzheimer's Association is at 919 North Michigan Avenue, Suite 1100, Chicago, Illinois 60611.

Stage 2. Very mild cognitive decline and perhaps memory lapses, forgetting familiar words or names, or maybe the location of their keys or eyeglasses or other objects. But these problems are typically not picked up by a medical examination or become apparent to friends or family.

Stage 3. Called mild cognitive decline. Friends and family may notice some memory or concentration deterioration which may be measurable in clinical testing or in a detailed medical interview in some, but not necessarily all, individuals. There can be a decline in the ability to plan and organize, or the inability to retain information that the patient has just read.

Stage 4. Called moderate cognitive decline or mild or early stage Alzheimer's disease. At this stage, a careful medical interview often detects clear cut deficiencies. This stage is characterized by a decreased knowledge of recent events and the ability to do mental arithmetic. There is a decreased capacity to do familiar tasks such as paying bills, managing finances, or planning meals. There may be withdrawal, especially in social and mentally challenging situations. It is often accompanied by reduced memory of their own personal history.

Stage 5. Moderately severe cognitive decline or moderate or mid-stage Alzheimer's disease. The patient requires some assistance with day-to-day activities and may forget their address or telephone number although they may still have knowledge of their own name and the names of their spouse or children. There may be confusion about where they are—or what day of the week it is. At this stage, the patient may need help in selecting appropriate clothing for the season or occasion, but they continue to be able to eat and toilet appropriately.

Stage 6. Severe cognitive decline or moderately severe or mid-stage Alzheimer's disease. This stage may be accompanied by significant personality changes. The patient may need extensive help with routine daily activities. Remembering things becomes even more difficult. The patient generally can recall his or her own name and distinguish familiar and unfamiliar faces, but may occasionally forget the name of his or her spouse. The patient may need supervision in dressing, even to details such as putting their shoes on the right feet. There may be a disruption of the normal sleeping and waking cycles. The patient may need assistance with the details of toileting, like flushing or wiping, and may have increasing urinary or fecal incontinence. They may wander and become lost. Personality changes at this point may include becoming suspicious or having delusions or hallucinations. There may be compulsive, repetitive behavior such as hand wringing.

Stage 7. Very severe cognitive decline or severe or late-stage Alzheimer's disease—the final stage of the disease. The patient loses the ability to speak but may still utter an occasional word or phrase. He or she becomes incontinent, and needs a great deal of help with eating, toileting, and other routine tasks. They can no longer walk or even sit without support, and are unable to smile or hold up their head. Swallowing may become impaired and reflexes become abnormal. There is weight loss even though the patient is eating well and having balanced meals.

As you can see, the disease becomes progressively worse as nerve cell degeneration takes place. Thinking, judging, and behavior are affected, and the damage eventually affects the control and coordination of physical movement.

Characterizing the different stages should provide a useful framework for how the disease may progress. It's important to remember that not all stages and related symptoms occur in every individual, and the transition from one stage to the next is usually not noticeable. However, these arbitrary benchmarks should help us understand the progression in general. How long does it take for this progression? People who are diagnosed with Alzheimer's live an average of nine years after their first diagnosis but the range may be anywhere from three to twenty years.

Because of the prevalence of this disease, there is a lot of information on the Internet about the symptoms and causes of Alzheimer's disease. Scientists do not fully understand what causes it, and there probably is more than one cause. Although age is the most important risk factor for Alzheimer's, scientists believe that family history is another risk factor in some cases. Much of the research so far has focused on blood circulation, and early evidence seems to indicate that high cholesterol and high blood pressure may increase the risk of developing Alzheimer's.

The Impact of Alzheimer's Disease on a Family

As you can see, the progression of Alzheimer's disease brings about an ever-increasing dependency for care. Since Alzheimer's disease is a degenerative disease of the brain a family will be severely impacted when someone in that family has the disease. Early stages of the disease don't cause a lot of disruption or require a lot of care. However, when the afflicted person is no longer able to perform familiar tasks, there can be problems. Someone with Alzheimer's might prepare a meal and not only forget to serve it, but might also forget that they even made it. Someone will need to provide assistance to the loved one who forgets where he or she lives and doesn't remember how to get home.

For the patient, his or her decline in memory and abstract thinking creates its own set of problems—for example, in managing personal finances. A person with Alzheimer's disease may put things in inappropriate places—keys in the silverware drawer, or books in a washing machine. Even these difficulties seem mild in comparison to what happens when personality changes, and the loved one become confused, irritable, suspicious, or fearful. Mood swings can occur rapidly with no apparent reason, and these unpredictable changes can cause a lot of stress in the family. When someone needs help with a basic task like eating or dressing, the help can be scheduled and life for the family can go on fairly normally. But when incontinence begins to occur, it will be necessary for the caregiver to be constantly available 24 hours a day. If the spouse is the only caregiver available, it puts a 24-hour-a-day demand on them, and soon, they will become physically and emotionally exhausted. There is added frustration for the caregiver because, even when it seems that he or she is doing everything possible to care for the loved one, the progression of the disease, and deterioration caused by it, just seem to continue. There is no way to control the disease process, and the caregiver will experience even more stress when he or she has to accept the continuing decline of the loved one for whom they are caring. When other members of the family become involved in providing care, there may be increased stress because they may not agree about the appropriate care needed.

Some family members may want to take care of their loved one at home, while others may believe that the best place for their loved one is in a facility where professional care is available around the clock. In the early stages, many people are not familiar with what resources for information and support are available in the community, nor do they have the skills and capabilities necessary to provide appropriate care, and this, too, adds to the stress. The caregiver may not know where or when to ask for help and may be afraid to seek professional help. Quite often, the caregiver neglects his or her own physical and emotional needs because he or she is totally consumed by the responsibility of caring for the loved one. The caregiver may forget to manage his or her own level of stress, and this creates complications for them. Stress can cause physical problems such as stomach irritation or high blood pressure, and it can cause changes in behavior and personality such as irritability and lack of concentration.

As the patient's need for care increases, they may very well need the skilled care that isn't available from family members. At that point, the family should discuss care options and make plans so that the transition from home to a nursing home will be easier. Add to that, the fact that the afflicted individual is often painfully aware of the losses and deterioration he or she is undergoing. Many Alzheimer's patients understand the progressive nature of the illness, and they do everything in their power to maintain their skills and abilities. Watching their loved one make these heroic efforts and still lose the battle to the disease is emotionally very difficult for family members and friends.

In their book, Alzheimer's Disease, subtitled The Family Journey, by Caron, Pattee and Otteson[13], the authors explore the impact of Alzheimer's disease on the family. They describe how the family can be understood as a system—as an identifiable entity that possesses a boundary, structure, and culture. They explain how families can marshal their resources to meet the challenges of taking care of a family member with Alzheimer's disease. They discuss the importance of planning to help families move from the reactive stance that responds only to the next problem or crisis into a proactive stance — into a stance that anticipates and responds to changing circumstances and emerging challenges.

Stress Issues of "Long" Long-Term Care

Alzheimer's disease, dementia, and every other disease that has a long duration causes more than the usual caregiver stress. Without appropriate planning and assistance by family members, caregivers become exhausted. It is different and a lot easier to give care for an hour each week for a month or two than it is to give ongoing care for years which seem to be endless.

---

[13] Wayne A. Caron, Ph.D., James J. Pattee, MD, and Orlo J. Otteson, MA.

That's why it is necessary to anticipate, locate, and schedule bringing in outside help as the circumstances dictate. Chapter 5 discussed these issues in more detail.

Depending on personal preferences or the wishes of the Alzheimer's patient, care may be provided in a facility. Many families rely on someone else to help them make the decision as to when is the time to move their loved one to a facility like a nursing home. Others make the decision when they can no longer continue to provide the services the patient needs. Once the family decides to use a facility like a nursing home, the next step is selecting one. Chapter 3 provides some help in selecting a nursing home.

Placing a loved one in a nursing home doesn't end the stress. In a study reported in the Journal of the American Medical Association[14] researchers measured the mental health of caregivers before and after a loved one was placed in a nursing home. They found that the already high depression and anxiety level before the loved one was placed in a nursing home did not change afterward. In fact, the use of anti-anxiety drugs actually increased slightly, and nearly half of the caregivers were at risk of clinical depression following the placement of their relative.

Personality Changes and Cognitive Impairment

Because of the special symptoms of dementia and

---

[14] Volume 292, No. 8, August 25, 2004, article entitled, "Long-Term Care Placement of Dementia Patients and Caregiver Health and Wellbeing" by Richard Schulz, Ph.D., etc., in JAMA, 2004, 292:961-967.

Alzheimer's disease—specifically, personality changes and cognitive impairment, it's important to look carefully at this aspect of the diseases. Because of the damaging process that occurs in the brain, the patient gradually loses control of language, reasoning, sensory processing, and thought. There may be restlessness, agitation, anxiety, tearfulness, and wandering. Hallucinations, delusions, suspicion, and paranoia may occur. Because of loss of impulse control, the patient may use vulgar language, become sloppy in their table manners, or even undress in inappropriate places and times. There may be groaning, moaning, or grunting. All of these negative changes in behavior by a beloved member of the family may be very difficult to watch and accept. It's important to stay calm, be patient, responsive, and flexible. That's not an easy assignment, and it will require a great deal of patience and self-control. Remember that the people with Alzheimer's disease may not be in control of their behavior but may be aware that they have lost that control, and that may be equally frustrating to them.

Communicating with your loved one may become very difficult. He or she may speak less and begin to use nonverbal gestures. When you're communicating with your loved one, use a calm tone of voice and avoid distractions like radio and television. Be careful not to interrupt the patient while he or she is speaking, and allow sufficient time for your loved one to process your question, formulate the answer, and then verbally respond. Speak slowly and clearly, maintaining eye contact, and use positive, friendly expressions. This advice is good advice not only for those afflicted with Alzheimer's disease, but for anyone that it is hard to communicate with.

Remember that simple tasks like getting dressed may become very challenging and frustrating for your loved one. Establish a specific time to dress and leave plenty of time so there's no need to rush or become impatient. Arrange the clothing in the order that the patient will put it on; that makes the task of dressing much easier. Also remember to select clothing that has easy-to-use Velcro closures rather than zippers or buttons.

Some people with Alzheimer's disease want to eat all the time, while others have to be encouraged to eat anything at all. A quiet atmosphere can help the person focus on the meal. Limiting the number of food choices and serving small portions can be helpful. If your parent or spouse struggles trying to use eating utensils, substitute finger foods and use a bowl instead of a plate.

Bathing can be a traumatic experience for some people suffering from Alzheimer's, while others have no problem with it. Telling the person each step of what you're going to do before and during the bath will help. Plan the bath at a time when the person is most likely to be calm.

The person who cares for a loved one at home needs to develop skills in feeding, skincare, bed baths, prevention of infection, lifting and transferring, and performing range of motion exercises. While doing all of this, it's important to look for signs that your loved one is becoming frustrated or agitated. If so, gently distract the person's attention to something else so that you can finish the task at hand. As you plan and establish a daily routine, be sure that there are activities that your loved one will enjoy in addition to bathing, meals and other daily tasks.

As we saw in the seven stages of Alzheimer's disease at the beginning of this chapter, changes in personality, emotions, and behavior usually become more apparent in the later stages of Alzheimer's disease. These changes may include delusions or obsessive behaviors, acute anxiety, and even violent behavior. At this stage, it's important to keep thinking of your loved one as an individual who can't control what's happening—that you aren't seeing the real person you've known and loved for all these years.

It is helpful to participate in a caregivers' support group which provides an opportunity and forum in which to exchange ideas, information, and even frustrations with people who are also caring for loved ones with Alzheimer's disease. Members of support groups offer each other caring and understanding because they know exactly what you're going through. You can contact your local Alzheimer's Association for a list of support groups in your area.[15]

Working your way through the difficulties of caring for your loved one with Alzheimer's can be terrifying. However, the better you understand it and its effects, the more likely you will be able to respond appropriately with care, love, and patience. Think about how much information is stored in a healthy brain, and then think about losing all of that information that has been gathered and learned over a lifetime. It's no wonder that your loved one may act like a two-year-old with highly aggravating or unusual behavior at times.

---

[15] Alzheimer's Association, 919 North Michigan Avenue, Suite 1000, Chicago, Illinois 60611. The phone number is 800-272-3900. The website is www.alz.org. The e mail address is info@alz.org.

Don't Go It Alone

Perhaps the best way to stay strong in the face of caring for your loved one with Alzheimer's disease is to hold a family conference. Don't hesitate or be reluctant to divide the burden of care so that things are less complicated and the work is spread more evenly. If it was not determined beforehand, decide now who the primary caregiver will be and who will make the final difficult decisions. Also, determine the best way for those people to keep the others informed. Talk about the guilt, anger, depression, and other feelings you have. Be open and honest, and accept them for what they are—feelings.

Make sure that you identify assets and financial records before the disease makes serious inroads. In the next chapter is a discussion of the legal documents you should have in place. If these haven't yet been taken care of, be sure they're done right away.

Keeping Your Loved One Safe

Safety is another issue. You will probably need to take steps that resemble baby proofing your home so that your loved one will be safe. Once Alzheimer's disease takes hold, the patient should no longer drive and potentially dangerous activities such as smoking must be eliminated for his or her own safety. Have them wear a sturdy ID bracelet with a name and phone number on it in case your loved one wanders away or becomes lost. See Chapter 5 for more details on making the home safe.

Respect the innate human dignity of your loved one, and provide opportunities for him or her to accomplish some tasks successfully, even if you have to simplify instructions taking them step by step, for simple tasks such as brushing teeth.

Care for Yourself

I'll say it again because it's so very important. Even though you're caring for someone else, you must also take care of yourself. Remember, you won't be able to provide good care unless you maintain your health and energy level. Be patient with yourself. Don't demand perfection of yourself or your patient. Cultivate a sense of humor so you can laugh rather than become frustrated when things aren't going right.

Ask for—insist on—help from others in your family or circle of friends. You need time off. You may be surprised to know that your family members and friends do care about you and do want to help. They may not know exactly what to do or how to do it, but if you ask, they probably will jump at the chance to care for you.

Chapter Eight

Legal Documents to Consider When Preparing for Incapacity

By Lori Skibbie, Esq.

"Failure to plan is planning to fail."

— Ross Kurcab

The information contained in this chapter is for informational purposes only and is not intended as legal advice. It can guide you through the relevant issues, but it cannot replace the personal counsel of a legal professional. You should contact an attorney in your area directly to obtain advice with respect to any particular legal issue or problem.

Before the need for long-term care is required, physical and mental capacity can diminish. Planning ahead for incapacity, by taking a few simple steps right now, can give you peace of mind. There are five legal documents that can help you prepare for incapacity.[16] Those five documents are: (1) Durable Power of

---

[16] All documents discussed in this chapter are based in Minnesota law only. If you live in a state other than Minnesota, please contact an attorney licensed in that state regarding proper preparation of these documents.

Attorney; (2) Health Care Directive; (3) Last Will and Testament; (4) Trust; and (5) Conservator and/or Guardian nomination.

Durable Power of Attorney

The durable power of attorney is a document through which you give another person the legal authority to assist you with the management of your financial matters. The person to whom you give that authority is called your attorney-in-fact. A durable power-of- attorney does not give away your right to manage your own finances while you have the capacity to do so. In fact, you can limit the powers of your attorney-in-fact. The benefit of the power of attorney is it remains effective if you become incapacitated and are unable to manage your assets without help. What makes a power of attorney durable is specifying in the document that you want the power-of-attorney to remain effective when you become incapacitated.

The risk of having a power-of-attorney is that your attorney-in-fact may have access to all of your assets and financial records. Therefore, you should choose your attorney-in-fact carefully, selecting someone you trust will manage your financial affairs in the same manner as you. Regardless of who you choose, attorneys-in-fact have a fiduciary duty to you and must manage your assets prudently.[17] Your attorney-in-fact must also keep complete records of all transactions they enter into on your behalf, and you can require your attorney-in-fact to submit accountings to you on a

---

[17] See Minnesota Statute § 523.21 (2004).

regular basis.[18] As further precaution, you can require your attorney-in-fact to be bonded.

Minnesota Health Care Directive

Many people are familiar with the terms "living will" and/or "health care power of attorney." These documents are typically used in combination to express a person's wishes for what types of medical treatment they do or do not want and who should make these decisions if they are unable to speak for themselves. In 1998, Minnesota revised its statutes to combine the two documents into a single document called a Health Care Directive.[19] This document is used to give another person the legal power to make medical decisions about your care if you are unable to do so. The person you name is called your health care agent and must be at least 18 years old or older to serve as your agent. For example, if you were in an accident and needed medical treatment but you were unconscious or unable to speak for yourself, your physician would telephone your health care agent who would then give instructions to the physician about your care or grant permission for certain types of medical treatment to be administered. In addition to who will make the decisions, your health care directive can also specify what medical treatments you would or would not want, whether you would prefer in-home, nursing home care, hospice care, etc., and into what facility or type of facility you would want to be admitted if you needed long-term care. A health care directive also allows you to specify if you want to be an organ donor, your funeral preferences, and if you prefer cremation rather than burial.

---

[18] Ibid.
[19] See Minnesota Statute § 145C (2004)

Having your wishes and instructions in writing may someday make it much easier for family and friends to make or agree on a decision for your treatment. As with the durable power of attorney, you will want to choose your health care agent very carefully. You want to be sure that you are choosing someone who understands and respects your health care decisions, to ensure your wishes are carried out exactly as you have specified in your health care directive.

Last Will and Testament

A Will is used for asset distribution upon your death.[20] Having a Will prepared does not, however, avoid probate, which is the legal process by which the court makes sure that your assets are properly distributed. Assets that are owned solely by you when you die are subject to probate. Assets that have a joint owner or named beneficiary are generally non-probate assets. For example, any bank accounts, automobiles, or real estate owned only in your name would be probate assets. A life insurance policy naming your estate as the beneficiary is also a probate asset. If any of the previously listed assets are owned in joint tenancy or have a named beneficiary, they are typically considered non-probate assets.

---

[20] Do not use your Will to provide detailed instructions regarding your funeral preferences, organ donation, or cremation. These are decisions which need to be made quickly and your Will may not be readily available, whereas your health care agent and your doctor should have a copy of your health care directive which should specify your preferences in these areas.

Trusts

There are two main types of trusts. The first type of trust is a testamentary trust which is established in your Will. The trust is funded with your assets upon your death. The assets of a testamentary trust, however, may be considered probate assets. A testamentary trust can be very specific as to the assets to be transferred into it, or it can generally accept assets of your estate that aren't otherwise specifically distributed. For example, you may own some life insurance policies, and you want them to be distributed to several beneficiaries instead of naming one specific beneficiary. You can name your estate as the beneficiary of the policies, and then specify in your Will that those certain policies be used to fund the trust. The trust will state how the assets of the trust are to be divided and distributed. Your Will also names a trustee who will be legally responsible for managing the trust and following the instructions you have set forth.

The second type of trust is a living trust. A living trust transfers your assets to a trust during your lifetime. You can be the trustee and manage the trust until such time as you may become incapacitated. The living trust allows you to name a successor trustee to take over management of the trust if and when you become incapacitated. The benefit of a living trust is the assets in a living trust are generally non-probate assets.

With a living trust, it is important to transfer all of your assets into the trust to avoid having those assets be subject to probate. You'll need to be sure you don't overlook or forget to transfer one small annuity account, for example, because that one asset may then be subject to probate.

Because assets need to be transferred to the trust, establishing a living trust can be more expensive to prepare than a Will. You should evaluate the value of your estate versus the cost to establish a trust. Those numbers will help you decide if creating a trust is a good strategy for you.

Conservator/Guardian Nomination Form

A conservator is a person appointed by the court with the legal authority to manage your financial affairs. A guardian is a person appointed by the court with the legal authority to make personal decisions for you. There is a simple form to be completed in which you nominate the person(s) you want to be your guardian and/or conservator should the need for either arise. The court appoints a guardian or conservator only in the event that there are no less restrictive alternatives available. If you have a power of attorney and/or a health care directive in place, you may not need to have a guardian or a conservator appointed unless it is determined that one or both of these documents is insufficient for the decisions that need to be made. For example, a health care directive wouldn't allow someone to take care of your personal property, where a guardianship would allow the person to make decisions about your personal property.

This nomination form is especially helpful for parents of a special needs child, or someone with a spouse who has special needs. For example, a wife has been caring for her husband at home when she suddenly has a massive stroke and ends up living in a nursing home. By completing a guardian nomination form, upon her incapacity there is someone nominated to serve as guardian for her husband. That person would then need to be confirmed by the court in order to have legal authority to act as guardian.[21]

An agent named in your health care directive is automatically nominated to be your guardian.[22] This is another good reason to be very careful about choosing your health care agent: if you should become incapacitated and need a guardian, the court will look at your health care directive to see who you have named as your health care agent. That person becomes a nominee to be your guardian. This can help avoid conflict within your family as it lets your family know your wishes about whom you want to be your guardian. Furthermore, you may avoid having the court appoint a stranger as your guardian because you will have exercised your freedom to choose a person you know and trust to take on these legal responsibilities.

Pre-Planning Your Funeral

In addition to the five legal documents, you may also want to pre-plan your funeral. You will have peace of mind knowing that the arrangements have been made and your family isn't left to decide what to do. You can make formal arrangements in writing with a funeral home using a pre-paid funeral plan, or you can simply prepare written instructions and put them with your Will and other important papers for your family members' reference. In your written instructions, you can be as detailed as you would like by specifying the

---

[21] See Minnesota Statutes §§ 524.5-301 and 524.5-302 (2004)
[22] See Minnesota Statutes § 145C.07, subd. 2 (2004)

music to be played, types of flowers, readings you may want, the funeral home you want to handle the arrangements, the church where you want the service to be held, the name of the pastor or priest to officiate, and any person you want to speak at the funeral service.

If you want to prepare for your funeral in advance, most funeral homes have pre-paid funeral plans available. Your Knights of Columbus insurance agent can help you set up a plan to pay for it.

It may be uncomfortable to think about your own funeral arrangements, but remember why you are doing this. By making all of the decisions and putting everything in writing, you are saving your loved ones from having to make difficult decisions during a very emotional time.

Medical Assistance Planning

Lastly, a brief note about medical assistance, Minnesota's version of Medicaid.[23] In Minnesota, the current political climate is to promote private pay for long-term care in order to reduce the number of recipients of government medical assistance benefits. The ultimate goal appears to be to have more citizens use their personal resources to pay for long-term medical care and assistance for as long as they are financially able.

---

[23] Medicaid is a federal welfare program under Title XIX of the Social Security Act. Medical assistance is Minnesota's Medicaid program under the federal program and Minnesota Statutes Chapter 256B.

To qualify for medical assistance, you have to have very limited assets and income. To get to the qualification thresholds, people will spend their nest eggs and/or transfer their assets to other family members. Before you start spending your assets and transferring property in an attempt to qualify for medical assistance, seek the advice of a qualified attorney. There are very specific rules and restrictions about transferring property and they must be followed to the letter. Otherwise you may find yourself in the situation where, for a period of time, you will not be eligible for medical assistance, yet you may not have any funds to pay for the care you need. This is a very complicated area of the law, and you should take the time to find an attorney for whom medical assistance planning is a major portion of their law practice. You may contact your local or state Bar Association for referrals.[24]

Lori D. Skibbie, Esq., is an attorney at the law firm of Steinhagen & Crist, P.L.L.P. in Minneapolis, MN, where she practices guardianship and conservatorship law, trust and probate administration, and estate planning.

---

[24] Hennepin County Bar Association Lawyer Referral: (612) 752-6666 or www.hcba.org

CHAPTER NINE

How to Pay for Your Long-Term Care

"A father can care for ten children better than ten children can care for one father."

— Old proverb

Did you expect to have an auto accident when you bought auto insurance? Did you expect to have a loss when you got your homeowners insurance? Do you think it's possible that you will have long-term care expenses to pay someday? If you don't think your children will pay for and take care of you when you need long-term care, then it's imperative that you start planning how to pay for it—the sooner, the better.

Do You Need Long-Term Care Insurance?

Maybe not.

Of people over age 65, almost half will spend some time requiring long-term care. Applicable research statistics follow.[25]

---

[25] Technical Report 1-01, Scripps Gerontology Center, Feb. 2001.

Diagram 9.1: Chances of Needing Care

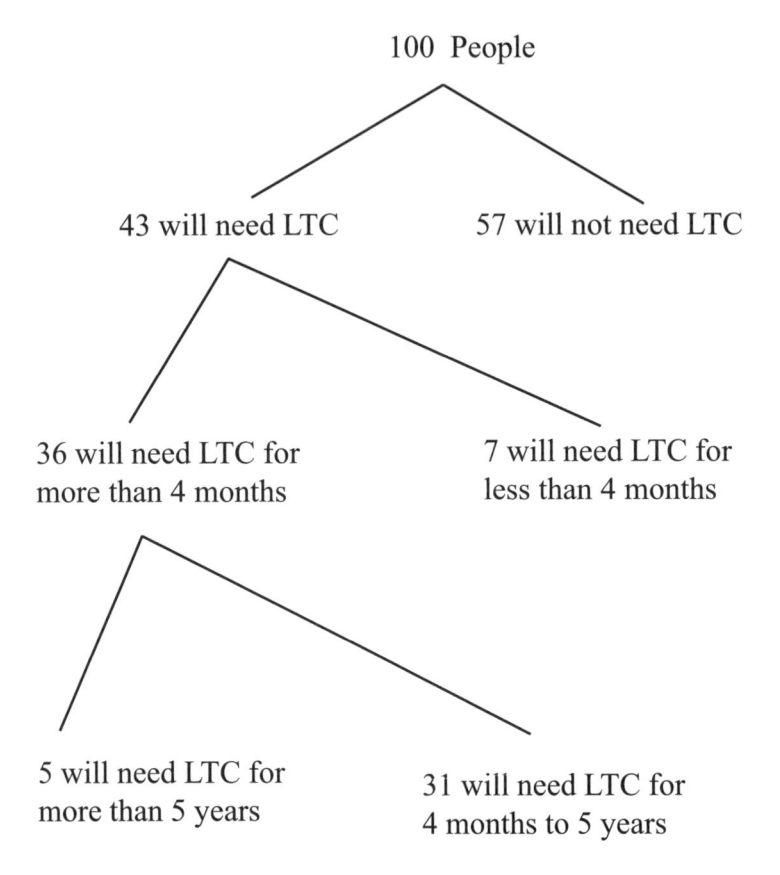

100 People

43 will need LTC   57 will not need LTC

36 will need LTC for more than 4 months   7 will need LTC for less than 4 months

5 will need LTC for more than 5 years   31 will need LTC for 4 months to 5 years

Financing long-term care should be approached with as much thought and preparation as any major expense. For some people, it is more expensive to pay for their long-term care than to purchase their home. With such a great risk, doesn't everyone need insurance? After all, the cost of long-term care can be $5,800 or more monthly. [26]

---

[26] Average annualized daily rate for a private room is $70,080 or $5,840 monthly. Average daily rate survey of all 50 states and the District of Columbia. MetLife Market Survey of Nursing Home and Home Care Costs, 2004.

The truth is that you may or may not need to buy insurance, and here's why.

Let's divide people into three groups:

1. Low Assets
2. Medium Assets
3. Large Assets

Low Assets: Members of this group have low net worth and may have difficulty making the annual premium payment for insurance. These people may be better off organizing their assets so that they can qualify for Medicaid. Medicaid only supports people once they have spent all but about $2,000[27] of their liquid assets. (This amount varies by state.) But there are ways to shelter assets from Medicaid so that you can get support without spending down your assets. Please note that Medicaid rules typically allow the healthy spouse to retain a residence, vehicle, and a modest amount of liquid assets for support. Since these rules vary from state to state, please consult an elder-care attorney regarding your specific situation.[28]

Medium Assets: The people in this middle group often need insurance. They have too much net worth to

---

[27] Most states have a $2,000 cap on assets, but a few go up to $4,000 and some are as low as $1,000. Average for all states is $2,146 as of January 21, 2004. Source: http://www.ltcconsultants.com/consumer/wyslyk/index.shtml

[28] The healthy spouse can typically protect between $18,132 and $90,660 or half of the couple's total assets, whichever is less. In addition to the amount previously mentioned, most states allow the healthy spouse to keep residential real estate and one motor vehicle. Society of Senior Certified Advisors, Working with Seniors: Health, Financial, and Social Issues, p. 334. December 2003.

qualify for Medicaid, yet they do not have enough assets to handle the expense of long-term care. Draining $5,800 or more per month for a private room from anyone in this group could erode their estate or, in the case of a married couple, could create an income hardship for the healthy spouse.[29] So, if you are in this group, seriously consider insurance. Insurance is a way to secure your financial independence. Often, long-term care insurance policies are for people who have significant assets that they want to preserve for family members, and to assure independence and not burden family members with nursing home bills.

Large Assets: Members of this group may have sufficient income and assets so that they can generally handle a monthly expense of $5,800 or more.[30] This group is also considered to have at least $75,000 in liquid assets. However, many of these people still do obtain insurance because it protects their estate from being depleted by a long-term care need. Most importantly, it gives them independence by providing a separate source of funds to be used only for long-term care expenses.

---

[29]On average, a senior citizen nursing home resident has lived there for about 2-1/2 years. As the average annual nursing home cost is believed to be about $50,000, the typical nursing home stay for an elderly person could deplete an estate by $125,000 or more over such time frame. Furthermore, the United Senior's Health Cooperative recommends the following guidelines for LTC insurance applicants: (1) no more than 7 percent of income should go toward premium, (2) retirement income should be at least $35,000, and (3) applicant should have assets of at least $75,000, not including the home and an automobile. Society of Senior Certified Advisors, Working with Seniors: Health, Financial, and Social Issues. pp. 212-226. December 2003.

[30] Society of Senior Certified Advisors, Working with Seniors: Health, Financial, and Social Issues, pp. 212-226. December 2003.

Risk Management: Essential for Financial Security

The concept of risk management is critical to your financial wellbeing. Risk management is simply the process of deciding which risks you're going to insure on your own and which risks you're going to transfer to an insurance company. Take a look at your overall insurance coverage and consider this question: Do I need each one of the policies I own, or should I self-insure? It's the only way to know whether the insurance you have is what you need—and to know that you do need the insurance you have.

Life expectancy continues to increase, which means we will have more people living longer and needing more years of long-term care. You have three options to deal with the issue:

1. **Go on Medicaid.** Medicaid is for people with few assets, although there are enough loopholes that almost anyone could qualify. For example, in many states, the primary residence is an "exempt" asset, which Medicaid cannot touch and which is not counted when determining Medicaid eligibility. That residence could be a 50-unit apartment building even though you only reside in one apartment. The entire building could be exempt. (Note: These rules and their implementation vary from state to state. Please check your state's rules at this web site: *http://www.aishealth.com/ManagedCare/MedCharts/MedicaidWeb.html.*) However, you probably don't want to be on Medicaid. It's been documented that Medicaid patients in some states get worse treatment in some

facilities than private pay patients.[31] You lose your independence with Medicaid.

2. **Buy Insurance.** Many people have obtained long-term care insurance to retain their independence. They don't want their beneficiaries making their health care decisions with assets from the general pool of their net worth. Sometimes family members can make less-than-optimal decisions when weighing how to spend their future inheritance. Since funds from a long-term care policy can only be used to pay for long-term care, it's a pot of money reserved solely for that use and cannot be derailed by family members or others.

3. **Self-fund.** Either keep $200,000 to $300,000 lying around, or have sufficient income to come up with the additional $4,000 to $6,000 per month when the need arises. Many people who can afford the cost still get insurance protection because they'd rather leave their assets to their beneficiaries than consume them for long-term care.

Medicaid As An Option

The younger you are, the more likely it is that changes are going to occur with existing government programs such as Medicaid and Social Security. The changes are going to be gradual, because our elected representatives are not going to make abrupt cuts in

---

[31] These two articles document this issue: *Kiplinger's Retirement Report (www.kiplinger/retreport/archives/1999/August/living.htm)* and the *National Senior Citizens Law Center Letter to Congressional Committee on Medicaid Discrimination (www.nsclc.org/mcaiddump.html)*.

programs in which many people are already receiving benefits or are about to begin receiving benefits.

So if you're looking at a program like Medicaid that the government has in place right now, keep in mind that, by the time you reach the age when you need long-term care, that program may be very different—with fewer benefits, more exclusions and new restrictions.

If you are "on the fence" and really think that your budget can't cover long-term care insurance—even as a portion of the protection you need—you may want to think seriously of spending down your assets so that you will qualify to receive benefits through Medicaid. Qualifying for Medicaid may consist of sheltering your assets. Remember, look-backs are in place. You would therefore have to take action far enough in advance of your actually needing Medicaid benefits so that recovery wouldn't be necessary.

If you are thinking about using this strategy, be sure to get professional advice and services from an elder-care lawyer who is experienced with appropriate state and federal laws and knows the process to protect your assets in this manner. Not just any lawyer will be able to help you.

If you are thinking of transferring your assets to your child and then having the child care for you when you need long-term care, beware! Besides the risk of having your money disappear through divorce or misappropriation, gambling, or other means, there are two other financial considerations.

One is that any earnings on the money will be taxed at your son or daughter's income tax rate, which could be higher than your own income tax rate in retirement. Additionally, if your son or daughter is holding your life savings, it could create a serious problem when your grandchildren apply for financial aid for college.

Here's another consideration. Your primary residence will not be counted in determining whether you're eligible for Medicaid. But it is one of your most <u>valuable</u> assets and therefore <u>most vulnerable to estate recovery after your death</u> if you had been receiving Medicaid benefits. In some states, when your Medicaid application is approved, a lien is placed on your home so that Medicaid will be able to recover—get back— some or all of the money they've spent for your care.

Insurance As An Option

You may be told that you have to have long-term care insurance. Not true. If you have enough assets, you could self-fund. If you are poor, you can get Medicaid. So who needs insurance? It's the 80% of the people in the middle who need it. So my caution to you is that you've got a substantial risk in your assets, which is this risk of long-term care. And if you don't think that having the protection of insurance is important, then consider these few questions.

Do you have auto insurance? You probably do. Your state may even require it. Do you have homeowners insurance? You probably have that, too. The risk of your house burning is 1 in 333. The risk of being in a car accident is about 1 in 8.

You've got insurance for those risks, though. The chance of your needing long-term care if you're over 65 is almost 1 in 2.[32] About half of the cases of long-term care continue for more than four months. Therefore, your chance of a prolonged illness is about 1 in 4 if you are over age 65.

Yet you have no insurance for that risk. So why don't people insure, knowing that this risk is so high—far higher than the risk of having damage to your car or your home? Because it's too costly? Actually, your homeowners insurance is also too costly. And so is your car insurance. I'll bet that you have never, ever had the thought when paying your insurance bill, "I love paying this insurance…It's so affordable." It's all too costly, isn't it?

Table 9.1: Chances of Life Risk Occurrences and Insurance Coverage for Risks

Risks in Your Life	Annual Chance of Occurence	Are You Insured?
House Burning	1 in 333	Yes
Car Crash	1 in 8	Yes
Medical Problem	Yearly?	Yes
Long-Term Health	43 in 100	?

Sources include: National Safety Council website, 2004; National Fire Prevention Association, 3/31/00; John Hancock website (http://www.gltc.jhancock.com/ltcbasics/quiz.cfm), 1/14/04; Fire Protection Agency, U.S. Census American Housing Survey, 6/03.

---

[32] Technical Report 1-01, Scripps Gerontology Center, February 2001.

What is really too costly is <u>not having the insurance</u>. What's too costly is what it will cost to pay the bills for care when you need to. What's too costly is when one spouse needs care and the other may be forced to decrease their standard of living to pay for it.

I would suggest to you that your homeowners insurance is far more costly than long-term care protection. You've paid your homeowners insurance all of your life, and the chances of you ever collecting on it are very small, because it's very unlikely—at least statistically—that your house will burn down or an airplane smash into it. That's expensive insurance because you'll most likely never need it.

If your assets are low, you want to think about organizing your affairs to get government support. If you're in the middle, you need to think about getting insurance. It's as simple as that. Actually, the insurance isn't too expensive. I'll tell you why most people don't have long-term care insurance. Most of what you learned about money, you learned from your parents. They had car insurance and homeowners insurance, and now so do you. Did they have long-term care insurance? No, and now neither do you. We simply repeat what we have learned.

But this is a new era. Your parents did not need long-term care insurance. In fact, it did not exist. Why didn't it exist? People did not live as long thirty years ago. Many just got sick and died because treatment was not available.

I predict those people who are in their 40s will now all have long-term care insurance by the time they reach 65. Why? Because they will have learned from their parents and observed the generation before them. It may even be built into the hospitalization policy.

How long will the average person live if he or she is 40 today? To the age of 90, 95, or 100? Such life spans will be common. So you are the transition generation. Your parents didn't need it. Your children will certainly need it, and you are right in the middle—the first group to live long enough to require long-term care protection.

Congratulations! You are the first generation to need this type of protection. Your generation is the first one to live this long, requiring you to have this risk to your assets that previous generations didn't have. Your life span will outlive your body's ability to support it in comfort.

If you end up deciding to pay your own way for long-term care from your own resources keep in mind that asset values may fluctuate. Make sure, also, that you are looking at their after-tax liquidation value if they're in qualified plans like IRAs or 401(k)s. Keep in mind the state and federal taxes you will have to pay when you use these. It can become complicated, so don't hesitate to work with an experienced CPA or accountant.

Let's look at some funding options that might be available to help you pay for long-term care or for long-term care insurance premiums.

Immediate Annuity

An Immediate Annuity is a contract purchased from an insurance company. You can make one lump-sum payment at the time of purchase, and the annuity then provides you with payments at regular intervals—monthly, quarterly, or annually for example. Many people purchase annuities so that they will have regular, predictable income after they retire.

Once you sign the contract for an Immediate Annuity and make the single payment required, you can immediately begin receiving payments. You can use some or all of your annuity payments to pay your long-term care insurance premium. Here's a hypothetical example.

> *A 70-year-old man makes a $20,000 single premium payment for an immediate annuity. He receives $1,900 a year for life from the annuity. (Annuity Shopper, 1/6/03). He uses this payment to make annual payments for his long-term care policy. At the end of his life, the annual payments stop, and none of the $20,000 he paid up front is returned to his heirs or to his estate.*

Please note that it's not within the scope of this book to present detailed information, explanations, and caveats about annuities. An annuity is mentioned here only to demonstrate how it could be part of an integrated financial plan and a possible strategy for paying long-term care insurance premiums.

Reverse Mortgage

Another source of revenue that you might consider as a way to pay for long-term care insurance is the reverse mortgage. This program allows people over the age of 62 to convert a percentage of the equity in their paid-off home to cash. A reverse mortgage is the opposite—or reverse—of the standard home mortgage that most of us are familiar with. Payments from a reverse mortgage company are paid into your pocket. The lender loans you the money and they will be paid back at the time of the sale of your home when you no longer reside there. As with other home-based loans, there are costs involved with reverse mortgages, and these fees can be added to your loan balance. Reverse mortgages can be used to pay for long-term care insurance or to pay for long-term care directly. They are not limited to this use; you can use the proceeds to pay for anything else you desire.

Again, please note that it's not within the scope of this book to present detailed information, explanations, and caveats about reverse mortgages. The concept of a reverse mortgage is mentioned here only to demonstrate how it could be part of an integrated financial plan and a possible strategy for paying for long-term care or for long-term care insurance premiums.

Savings to Cover Expenses

Some people ask me if they would be better off putting money away to prepare for the need for long-term care rather than investing in insurance. It sounds like a good idea, but it's unlikely that you could save enough to equal what the insurance policy would pay.

Let's say that at age 45 you start saving $1,110 per year for your future long-term care needs. With your savings hypothetically returning 5 percent annually, you would accumulate $57,786 over 25 years. That would bring us to the year 2030. But in 2030, the cost of the average stay in a nursing home could be over $495,000.[33] Instead, if you were to invest the same amount of money in a long-term care insurance policy, it would provide benefits of $529,980 for Comprehensive Care coverage in your home, in an assisted living facility, or a nursing home.[34]

What About Waiting Until Later?

The annual premium for someone who purchases an insurance policy described above at age 45 is $1,107.97, and that amount is not scheduled to go up as you get older.

If you purchase the same Comprehensive Care policy **at age 55**, the annual premium would be $1,504.63. If you purchase it **at age 65,** the premium is $2,346.76 annually.

Waiting until you are **age 75** to purchase this policy, you would pay an annual premium of $5,410.97 annually. If you decide to buy the policy at **age 85**, the annual premium would be $8,765.88. These rates were in effect on May 31, 2005 and are shown for comparison purposes only.

You can see why it's important to obtain long-term care insurance as early as possible. The longer you wait, the more expensive it gets.[35] It is also wise to purchase a policy when you're young and in good

---

[33] Source: Federal LTC Insurance Program Brochure, Jan. 2004.
[34] Based on a Knights of Columbus Comprehensive Care policy of a married person with $150 per day coverage, 5 percent compounded inflation rider, 90-day elimination period, and a 15 percent spousal discount. The costs for the policies are for Minnesota residents.

health so that you can qualify for coverage. As we age and the possibility of developing adverse medical conditions becomes greater, we run a growing risk that we will become <u>uninsurable</u>—that we won't be able to qualify for insurance. If you want protection, apply now rather than later.

Does that mean that if you're already age 75 you wouldn't be able to qualify to buy long-term care insurance? Not necessarily. Insurance companies accept many pre-existing medical conditions. To find out for sure, go ahead and apply. There's no cost to you to make an application. Chapter 10 will provide you with more information on how to qualify and what options of coverage are available.

Two Important Reasons to Get Long-Term Care Insurance

If you were to get sick and need help, who do you think would care for you? If you're married, you could turn your spouse's life upside down—from an easy retirement to a dreary existence.

If you are single, your children may get the burden. They may either feel obligated to try and help you by fitting you into their already busy schedule, or they may resent caring for you, although they would never say so.

Or you could deplete your assets—your nest egg—the money that would otherwise have gone to your heirs some day. Therefore, it's important to realize that a

---

[35] Ibid.

major reason to get long-term care insurance is to protect your family.

The other reason is to preserve your independence. Do you want your children helping you brush your teeth? Do you want family members deciding how to spend your assets to pay for your care? Insurance provides a separate asset that can be used only to pay for quality long-term care for you. You can use it to get quality care from professional caregivers. Whether the care is given inside or outside your home, insurance can help you keep your independence.

The bottom line is that, not only do you <u>maintain independence</u> and <u>preserve your personal assets</u>, but you also build in <u>flexibility</u>. Because the policy can provide <u>protection against inflation</u>, you won't have to worry about the increasing costs of long-term care services in the years ahead. **Wouldn't you like to protect your wife or husband or children in this way?**

Choices and Flexibility

When <u>you</u> are paying the bills for your health care—whether you're using your own funds or your long-term care insurance policy—you have choices. You can choose to have a private or semi-private room. If you're unhappy or uncomfortable in a particular nursing home or assisted living facility, you could simply pack up and move to another facility, or you could change where you're getting your care. But if someone else—that is, Medicaid—is paying your bills, <u>you never have those options</u>. They will tell you where you will receive your care and that's that.

Since long-term care is so expensive and Medicaid so limiting, most middle-income people who qualify for long-term care insurance are very wise to make this purchase. Without insurance and without sufficient savings, assets, or resources, they may be forced to downgrade their lifestyle and rely on restrictive, uncertain government programs. They risk the loss of dignity and, of course, their independence.

Building Economic Independence

You can improve your potential for long-term economic independence if you're still working. Invest wisely. Conserve capital. Live within your means. Take full advantage of benefit plans available through your employer, in which you make contributions that your employer matches.

You may want to increase your savings late in your career and possibly work two to three years longer than you had originally planned in order to increase the principal in your accounts. Retirement in the 21st century is a process or transition rather than an ending.

According to the 2002 study by the National Council on Aging, Inc., 42 percent of people 65 and over say they are **retired and working** or **not retired at all.** Many continue to generate income in a second career that gives meaning to their lives and enhances their financial accounts.

Information on the website of the U.S. Office of Personnel Management *(www.ltcfeds.com)* shows how long-term care is paid for now:

Table 9.2: Who Pays for Long-Term Care?

	Home Care Costs	Nursing Home Costs
Private Long-Term Care Insurance	5.0%	5.0%
Medicare	15.3%	8.0%
Medicaid	17.3%	41.0%
Out-of-Pocket	62.2%	46.0%

What Will It Cost?

So far I've shared some general costs of long-term care. To get a better handle on what will have to be funded if we need long-term care, let's start with the average cost of nursing homes in the United States—about $143 per day.[36] As you might expect, <u>costs vary considerably from location to location.</u> On the website of the U.S. Office of Personnel Management mentioned above, the average costs in <u>Minneapolis, MN</u> are currently:

Home health care services - $23.60 per hour

Assisted living facility - $2,090.85 per month

Nursing home - $130.08 per day

Compare those rates with ones for Shreveport,

---

[36] Met Life Mature Market Institute, "Met Life Market Survey on Nursing Home and Homecare Costs 2002," April 2002.

Louisiana. Home health care services there average $12.80 per hour—about half of the rate in Minneapolis. The monthly rate for an assisted living facility in Shreveport is $1,380, and the daily charge for a nursing home is $84.13. I've given these examples to show the range of costs for similar categories of services and facilities. You can find rates for your location by visiting the website of the U.S. Office of Personnel Management: *www.ltcfeds.com*.

What's Around the Corner?

I don't know of anyone who can accurately predict the future, but that doesn't mean that our hands are tied regarding long-term care. The best strategy seems to be to put a long-term care plan in place. If you don't already have such a plan, or if you believe that your needs, goals, or risk tolerance have changed since you put a plan in place, <u>now is the time</u> to review how you will deal with this potential expense in your life and take some actions.

Realize that long-term care is <u>not</u> only for your parents or someone else. It's <u>not</u> even just for people nearing retirement age, since a serious injury or illness requiring extended long-term care can strike <u>any one</u> at <u>any age</u> at <u>any time</u>. Even if you don't make your plans today, you can start getting the information you'll eventually need.

If you're wondering whether long-term care insurance is financially appropriate for you, my advice is: If you can afford the premiums without having to drastically change your lifestyle, you should go ahead and buy it. To do that, you'll need to understand what types of policies, plans, and options are available and which would best fit your needs and desires. In Chapter 10 we'll look at those choices so you can get a general idea of what the premiums are for a plan that's appropriate for you. After reviewing that, if you feel that you can afford it, you probably can. Most people know exactly what they can and can't afford.

Unique Coverage and Benefits

Long-term care insurance is unique. It's the only insurance designed to help cover the costs of <u>long</u>-term care services. Health insurance and disability insurance do <u>not</u> cover custodial care—that is, the care needed to perform the activities of daily living. Without long-term care insurance, chances are very good that you'll be responsible for paying most of the costs out of your own pocket.

The amount of insurance and type of coverage you need can be determined by a fairly comprehensive review of what's available and what you want. It's probably not something you could do on your own because it's a complex process, and you may overlook some of the factors or miscalculate some of the figures you need to make the right decision.

The only appropriate way that I know of to conduct an accurate, comprehensive review and analysis of your individual situation is with a trained professional, such as an insurance agent from the Knights of Columbus. The agent will work with your current and projected future income and will calculate the current and future costs of providing long-term care locally. The agent will also help you decide which costs, levels of care, and optional services you want the policy to cover. If you don't know how to contact your local field agent, go to *www.kofc.org* on the web. Click on "Find an Agent". Then enter your ZIP code to find the right person to contact.

Budgeting for Long-Term Care Insurance

Purchasing long-term care insurance requires planning to fit the premium payments into your budget. There are numerous ways to fund premium payments. You may use current earnings or interest from funds that you have available. Dividends and annuity income can be additional sources. If you have one or more cash value life insurance policies of adequate size, you could use them as a source to pay for your long-term care. You may even decide that a combination of long-term care insurance coverage and using personal savings to pay for some of your long-term care expenses is best for you. Just keep in mind that <u>delaying the purchase of an insurance policy will increase the amount of the premium you'll pay</u>. For instance, you may find that waiting from age 55 to age 65 will <u>double</u> your annual premium. Even though you may be paying the higher premium for fewer years, your total cost will end up being higher.

Five Ways to Potentially Reduce the Cost of Long-Term Care Insurance

While it would be ideal to have complete coverage—inflation protection, lifetime coverage, at least $160/day benefit—it is better to have at least a basic policy than to have none at all. In other words, a minimum policy is better than being uncovered for the high cost of long-term care. In order to help you minimize the cost of insurance, there are some ways to reduce the cost while still having basic coverage. No one knows when a health catastrophe can strike. An onset of a heart attack, stroke, cancer, Parkinson's and Alzheimer's disease are debilitating illnesses which give no advanced warning. Protect yourself and your family financially.

Here are five ways to get covered at a lower cost:

1. **Reduce the coverage period.** For example, reduce the term of the policy from lifetime to five years or from five years to three years. Savings can be significant, and a three-year policy covers the majority of the cases requiring long-term care.[37]

2. **Reduce the daily benefit.** If the actual cost of nursing care is $192 per day[38] and you cover just $130 or $160 per day with insurance, some people can make up the difference with other income sources, such as Social Security or interest income.[39]

3. **If you are age 75 or over, consider omitting the inflation protection.** Although you will hopefully never need long-term care, if you do, you could need it within ten years—by age 85. Therefore, you

---

[37] Long-Term Care Study, Michigan State University, 2004.
[38] Average daily rate survey of all 50 states and the District of Columbia. MetLife Market Survey of Nursing Home and Home Care Costs, 2004.

do not need to protect for inflation over as long a period as, for example, a 65-year-old would need to prepare.

4. **Consider partial home care coverage.** By reducing the benefits for home care, you can lower your premium. As an example, get $100/day benefit for Facility Only Care payments and $50/day for Comprehensive Care payments. (Home care costs can be less expensive if you have family or friends who can help with care.)

5. **Eliminate home care insurance.** Many people have a spouse or friends or relatives who can assist them in the home. Hired home aides are relatively inexpensive ($18 per hour).[40] Care at home may easily be covered within the means of your own income. The most important coverage to obtain then is for care outside of the home.

Long-term care costs are more than financial. The National Coalition on Aging found that the <u>average time spent providing hands-on care to a sick or disabled relative now exceeds 41 hours per week</u>,[41] the equivalent of a second full-time job. With Medicare covering only a fraction of long-term medical expenses, many families have to dip into their own savings to see

---

[39] If you have sufficient interest income or Social Security income, it may be better for you to insure for the majority of the cost of long-term care and self-insure for the remainder. This has the effect of lowering the current cost of the insurance premiums without subjecting you to being unable to cover the costs of long-term care, if and when they arise.

[40] Average hourly rate, MetLife Market Survey of Nursing Home and Home Care Costs, August 2004.

a parent through an extended period of care. So it's not just paying for your own long-term care that may impact your life.

It's not surprising, then, that many adult children are taking charge. They're addressing the issue of their parents' future needs today by purchasing long-term care insurance on their parents' behalf. In Chapter 10, there is information about the Knights of Columbus affiliation with LifePlans to provide help and discounts for family members just by having a Knights of Columbus policy yourself. Parents and other relatives, including children, are covered by these discount programs at no additional cost to you.

Should You Buy Long-Term Care Insurance?

No, you shouldn't buy long-term care insurance if you can't afford the premiums, because you'll need to keep paying annual premiums until you actually begin to receive care.

You shouldn't buy long-term care if you're already receiving Medicaid.

If your only source of income is Social Security benefits for Supplemental Security Income (SSI), you should not buy long-term care insurance.

If you often have trouble paying for necessities (utilities, food, medicine, and other important needs) you should not buy long-term care insurance.

---

[41] The NCOA/John Hancock Long-Term Care Survey, March 1999

Some people say that they want to leave the largest possible inheritance to their beneficiaries, and so they don't want to spend any of their money on long-term care insurance premiums. But that's short-sighted and counterproductive. Without any insurance, the cost of long-term care can have a devastating effect on your estate. Will your money last as long as your life?

Long-term care insurance may be a lousy deal, but right now it's just about the <u>only</u> deal that you can rely on.

It all boils down to risk management and **making long-term care a definable expense rather than a blank check.** When you buy the insurance, you know the cost. If you don't buy the insurance, you are taking on the risk and you are self-insuring for it. That can be much more devastating. In the next chapter, we will look at long-term care protection, what it covers, and what it costs.

"We're so sorry Grandma, but..."

Chapter Ten

All About Long-Term Care Insurance

> "It is a strange anomaly that men should be careful to insure their houses, their ships, and their merchandise, and yet neglect to insure their lives; surely the most important of all to their families and more subject to loss."
>
> —Benjamin Franklin

If you agree with Benjamin Franklin's advice, you will want to read the rest of this chapter and protect yourself. On the other hand, if you are willing and able to write a check each month for as long as necessary to pay for long-term care—and if it doesn't bother you to be writing all of these big checks—then you don't need long-term care insurance.

In order to get the right coverage, once you decide that you need insurance, you will have a number of <u>things to consider and choices to make</u>. This chapter will help you learn about your options and simplify your course of action.

It's Not Easy...

Buying long-term care insurance is not as easy as buying life insurance. First of all, we all know that we're going to die. But we <u>don't</u> know whether we'll ever need long-term care, or for how long. We do know, though, that if we have to pay for the care, it will be expensive. In Chapter 9 we discussed the concept of risk management—the basis of modern financial planning. You practice good risk management when you decide how to protect yourself from the financial risk of paying for long-term care.

This chapter will provide information about Knights of Columbus long-term care insurance as a way to manage your risk. Not every detail can be presented here so call your Knights of Columbus insurance agent to get additional information you need. It's important to be educated and aware. You will want to work with a professional who can explain all of the options, answer all of your questions, work out the math to project future costs of care and costs of various types of coverage. Your insurance agent can help you select the best care plan to meet your needs. He is a trained professional who can be your best ally in making the right decisions. If you choose hastily or without guidance, you may find out twenty or thirty years later—when you need the insurance—that the policy doesn't provide the coverage or pay for the services you need then. Knowing that you chose the plan that's best for you because you had an expert help you gives you peace of mind.

I cannot tell you what is right for you regarding long-term care insurance. I can only stimulate your thinking about the concept and potential need. I will <u>encourage you to plan ahead for what you want</u>, share those plans with your family, and <u>take action now</u> so you will have the funds, to pay for the plans you have made. Make sure you understand all the provisions of any policy that you purchase. Discuss the policy with family members and others whose opinions you respect, and don't be pressured into making quick decisions. Even if you never need to fund long-term care, you'll feel great—and have a sense of relief—being prepared and knowing that your needs will be met. **In a nutshell, the right long-term care insurance will give you long-term peace of mind.**

Don't Wait Until You Need It

You know that you can't buy auto insurance to cover an accident <u>after</u> the fact. You know that you can't buy life insurance once your doctor tells you you have a terminal illness. It's the same with long-term care insurance and, unfortunately, <u>too many people wait until it's too late</u> before they decide to apply for it.

It may seem complicated to decide what kind of long-term care insurance coverage to buy. I can assure you that it is no more complicated—in fact, it's <u>less complicated</u>—than buying auto insurance. If you look at all the options available in an auto insurance policy and then have someone like your teenage son or daughter decide which of those options and how much coverage is needed, they would find it difficult to make the right choices for an appropriate policy without your help or the help of a knowledgeable agent. It's the same with long-term care insurance. Fortunately, you don't have to know, understand, analyze, and compare all of the options available for long-term care insurance all on your own. You can rely on the expertise of a Knights of Columbus insurance agent who knows the products, the options, the applications, and the restrictions inside and out. Together, it will be straightforward to determine what coverage and what options would give you the protection you want for yourself. It becomes much more simple.

What Exactly Will You Need?

The average length of stay in a nursing home is 2.6 years.[42] Deciding what the average long-term care cost is going to be years from now is like deciding what the average auto accident will cost then. It's impossible. Costs may seem high, but consider the services that this insurance provides, including your personal care by health professionals and other service delivery agents. Consider the assurance you and your family have that you will maintain a quality of life while you receive the needed care and rehabilitation. Consider that you will be in a safe, supportive environment to maintain or achieve the highest level of independence possible. Consider that your spouse or other family members won't have to be burdened with the expenses of paying for your care or with the burden of caring for you because there's no money to hire caregivers. For what you get, do the costs for this insurance still seem high?

Genealogy can be a key factor for determining coverage and predicting your possible future needs for long-term care. For example, research shows that if there is Alzheimer's disease in your family history you are more likely to experience dementia and Alzheimer's disease. That may be a factor for you in determining how much or how long or what type of coverage you may need someday.

---

[42] Conning and Company, "Long-Term Care Insurance — Baby Boom or Bust," 1999

Financial Health and Stability of Insurer

You'll want to choose an insurance company with long-time financial stability and security—a good indicator that the company will still be around and financially capable of paying any claims you may submit years from now.

There are more than 110 companies now offering long-term care insurance products, according to the Health Insurance Association of America. Not all companies are authorized to sell long-term care insurance in every state. The Knights of Columbus has this approval in all states.

If you're not eligible to apply for long-term care insurance with the Knights of Columbus, be sure to investigate the financial strength of the insurers you are considering before making any decisions or purchases. Look for ratings from the insurance rating services such as A.M. Best or Standard & Poor's. You can find these rating services in the reference section of your library or call A.M. Best at 908-439-2200 or Standard & Poor's at 212-438-2000.

With an appropriate long-term care insurance policy in hand, you can sleep easier knowing that you've made a smart move to protect your hard-earned assets and your ability to make the choices that are most important to you. With a Knights of Columbus long-term care insurance policy, you get even more protection and assurances. You get the stability, reliability, and the expertise of a company that's been insuring individuals for more than 120 years. Later in this chapter we will discuss how family members of Knights of Columbus policyholders also can benefit through their eligibility for discounts for long-term care products and services.

Designing the Right Policy for You

You should not settle for a "one size fits all" long-term care insurance policy. There are choices to be considered and decisions to be made so that the end product will be a "fit" for you, your family, and your budget. Let's consider some of these choices to see how they might fit your needs and address your concerns.

How long do you wish to be covered? The longer amount of time you want to be covered, the higher the price tag. Policies covering three or five years will have lower premiums than lifetime coverage, which is the most expensive. The trade-off is that lifetime coverage will provide for the costs of nursing home or home healthcare for as many years as you need it.

The price of long-term care insurance is based on your age at the time you buy it. The younger you are when you purchase a policy, the less expensive the annual premiums will be. With the Knights of Columbus plans, the premium you pay stays level each year, unless premiums are increased for all policyholders at once and the increases have been approved by state regulators. So even though you keep getting older and closer to the time when you may need long-term care, the premiums don't keep going up every year as they may do with other types of insurance—for example, annual renewable term life insurance.

There is no one "best policy." That's why it's essential to work with an experienced agent to custom-make a policy that affordably fits your lifestyle and future needs, taking into consideration how much insurance to buy and which options you want.

"Short and Fat" vs. "Long and Thin" Policy

One way to look at long-term care insurance coverage would be to consider a policy that provides a larger daily benefit for three or five years — a policy that's "short and fat" –rather than one that provides a smaller daily benefit for your lifetime—called "long and thin."

Long-term care premiums for men and women are the same at the same age. So let's look at three options for someone who is 55 years old right now. Please note that the annual premiums shown in this example are for a Knights of Columbus "Facilities Only Care" long-term care insurance policy with a 90-day elimination period and an inflation rider.

One policy offers a benefit of $150 a day for three years. The second policy offers a benefit of $120 for five years. The third offers a benefit of $110 for a lifetime. All of the policies have compound inflation riders that increase the daily benefit 5 percent per year.

The annual premium for the three-year policy is $1,104.60. The five-year policy has an annual premium of $1,105.56. The lifetime policy has an annual premium of $1,106.60. **The annual premiums for these three different policies are essentially the same.**

Table 10.1: "Short and Fat" vs. "Long and Thin" Policy Comparison (rates at age 55)*

Benefit Duration	Benefit Per Day	Annual Premium	Benefit Per Day at Age 85	Total Available
3 Years	$150	$1,104.60	$617	$675,615
5 Years	$120	$1,105.56	$494	$901,550
Lifetime	$110	1,106.60	$453	$2,480,175 (At 15 Years)

*Refers to a Knights of Columbus "Facilities Only Care" insurance policy at age 55 with a 90-day elimination period and inflation protection rider (5% compounded annually).

Actuarial tables indicate that a **policyholder is most likely to need long-term care at age 85**—thirty years down the road for our 55-year-old. Let's look at the benefits at that time. The $150 three-year policy will have grown and will then make available $617 per day. The $120 per day, five-year policy will have grown and make available $494 per day, and the lifetime policy starting at $110 per day will be making available benefits worth $453 a day.[43]

Although the premiums are roughly the same each year over the same 30-year period, we're able to see the differences between the policies when we calculate the total amount these three policies would pay out. The three-year policy would pay out a maximum of $675,615. The five-year policy would pay out $901,550 maximum, while the lifetime policy would provide unlimited dollars. An Alzheimer's patient could require as much as fifteen or more years of care from the time the diagnosis is made. If that is the case,

---

[43] These figures are provided for comparison purposes only.

the lifetime policy would pay out $2,480,175 over a fifteen-year period, and it would still be available to pay more if the patient lives even longer.

Since the annual premiums for the three different policies vary by only $2 per year, the total expense for coverage for the thirty-year period from age 55 to 85 would be $33,188 for the three-year plan, $33,166.80 for the five-year plan, and $33,198 for the lifetime plan.

If you use the maximum benefit provided by any of them—even the three-year coverage plan—**you leverage your premium dollars more than 20 times.**

Which plan and approach best meets your needs and desires—the "short and fat," the "long and thin" or the "one in the middle?" The annual premiums are all about the same, so you can **compare them based on what each provides rather than what each costs.**

With a 5 percent annual increase for inflation, in 30 years the average cost of nursing home care of $143 per day today, would be $589 per day. If you have an inflation rider with your policy and the actual rate of inflation is <u>less</u> than 5 percent so you <u>don't need</u> all of the benefit dollars per day that you have available, the benefit dollars per day that you <u>have available but don't use</u> are actually "banked" for you. Those extra dollars are used to extend the length of your coverage if you have a three- or five-year coverage policy.

You may be wondering how premiums compare at the same age for 3 year, 5 year and lifetime policies with the same coverage per day. Table 10.2 below shows the differences.

Table 10.2: Comparison of 3 Year, 5 Year and Lifetime Policies (Rates for $150 Per Day at age 55)*

Benefit Duration	Annual Premium	Benefit Per Day at Age 85	Total Available
3 Years	$1,104.60	$617	$675,615
5 Years	$1,381.95	$617	$1,126,025
Lifetime	$1,509.00	$617	$3,378,075 (At 15 Years)

* Refers to a Knights of Columbus "Facilities Only Care" insurance policy at age 55 for $150 per day with a 90-day elimination period, and inflation protection rider (5% compounded annually).

What's Next?

Are you wondering how to get long-term care insurance and what is involved in qualifying for it? The first step is to tell your Knights of Columbus insurance agent. Call him to set up an appointment. When you get together you can work out the details of what you need. The agent will ask you several questions about your health that may determine your eligibility to buy a policy. When the insurance company's underwriter looks at your application, he or she reviews the medical and health-related information you have provided to determine if you present an acceptable level of risk and are insurable. There will be a telephone interview or perhaps a personal interview with a nurse. There may also be a review of your medical records. Therefore, when you apply for coverage, you will be asked to sign a release giving your permission to the insurance company to have access to your medical records.

<u>Be sure to answer all medical-related questions honestly</u>. If you make a false statement, it could mean that your policy will be cancelled retroactively back to when it was issued. **So don't let anyone convince you to lie about your medical condition.**

The Cost of Waiting

Waiting until later to buy long-term care insurance can result in a deterioration of health that can prevent you from qualifying for coverage. Additionally, the table below illustrates the cost of waiting to buy the insurance. Note the costs of the annual premium at the different ages. If the premiums are paid until age 85, when care may be needed, the total cost of premiums increases more than two and one-half times from age 45 to age 75. When you see the need for long-term care insurance, you would be wise not to wait to get it.

Table 10.3: The Cost of Waiting to Buy[44]

Age Policy Bought	Annual Premium	Total Paid by Age 85
45	$339.60	$13,584
55	$578.00	$17,340
65	$1,161.40	$23,228
75	$3,431.30	$34,313

---

[44] Annual premiums are based on the following assumptions: Knights of Columbus Comprehensive Care policy, $100.00 daily benefit, five-year benefit duration, 90-day elimination period. For comparison purposes only.

If You Don't Qualify...

Insurance agents are not trained as underwriters and so your agent will not be able to give you a definitive, final answer about whether you will qualify for coverage or not. Health conditions that may cause you to be declined for long-term care insurance include Parkinson's disease, Alzheimer's disease or other dementia, multiple sclerosis, osteoporosis if it has resulted in fractures, muscular dystrophy, diabetes with complications such as eye problems or amputation, ALS (Lou Gehrig's disease), heart disease, cancer or blood disorders, height and weight outside of chart limits, and any other condition that already requires you to have help with dressing, bathing, and walking.

Many other health conditions could be allowable depending on your particular situation. By itself, smoking is not considered a problem. However, it could become a problem in conjunction with other conditions like emphysema. High blood pressure may not be a problem if it is well managed and controlled, but if it's not under control, it might cause someone's application to be declined.

Sometimes, over time, conditions improve and that may mean that an applicant may qualify at a later time. Postponement may be necessary until a health condition has improved to the point where it is clearly not a problem. Your agent will discuss your situation with you, with the help of pre-qualification questionnaires prepared by the Knights of Columbus Insurance Underwriting Department.

Two Types of Policies Available

The Knights of Columbus offers two types of long-term care insurance policies. There is one called a **Facilities Only Care** policy that covers long-term care in nursing homes and other types of assisted living facilities. It pays 100 percent of the expenses you incur for care rendered in a long-term care facility, hospital long-term care unit, or assisted living facility, up to your maximum monthly benefit and maximum lifetime benefit.

The second is called a **Comprehensive Care** policy. Its coverage is broader and includes home health care services, adult daycare, homemaker services, hospice care, care management, alternative care, bed reservation, caregiving training, home modification, respite care benefit, and a transportation benefit. The **Comprehensive Care** policy coverage is home and community based. It pays 100 percent of the expenses you incur for home health care services, adult daycare, homemaker services, or hospice care that is given in your home or community facility up to your maximum monthly benefit and maximum lifetime benefit. It covers in-home care and everything covered by a Facilities Only Care policy.

If you want to have care available to you in your home, you will need the **Comprehensive Care** policy. If, on the other hand, you want to be in a facility for your care, you would purchase **Facilities Only Care** policy.

Both types of Knights of Columbus long-term care policies have guaranteed renewability. Benefits cannot be cancelled if you pay premiums when they are due.

Premiums will be waived during the period in which you are receiving benefits. The following information applies to both policy types:

You can **choose a daily benefit** amount from $50 to $250, in increments of $10. The **maximum monthly benefit** is the daily benefit amount multiplied by 30. The **maximum lifetime benefit** is the daily benefit amount multiplied by 365, and that's multiplied by the benefit duration you choose. "Benefit duration" refers, of course, to the length of time your policy covers. **You can choose three years, five years, or lifetime.**

There is an "elimination period" or "waiting period," similar to having a deductible, referring to the length of time you'll have to wait before you begin receiving benefits from the policy. You will be responsible for paying for any and all care you receive during the elimination period. **You can choose an elimination period of 30, 60, 90, or 180 days.**

For home or community based benefits, your **lifetime elimination period will be reduced by half** if you follow a plan of care prescribed for you by one of our approved care managers. A care manager approved by the Knights of Columbus prescribes and periodically reviews an appropriate plan of care for you. Otherwise, your lifetime elimination period remains the same.

In most states, when you purchase a Knights of Columbus long-term care insurance policy, you will be eligible to receive a discount if you also purchase a policy for your spouse.

One option available to a couple purchasing policies is called the **"shared care" benefit.** When both spouses have identical policies and one uses up all of the benefits available in his or her own policy, he or she can then use the benefits available through the other spouse's policy. Upon the death of one spouse, the remaining benefits are transferred to and can be used by the surviving spouse.

If the couple does **not** choose the shared care benefit, they can instead choose to receive a 15 percent discount on their premiums. If both spouses are not covered, either because one doesn't qualify or does not desire coverage, there is a 10 percent discount available.

Protection against inflation is available through the Knights of Columbus policies. There are two options you can choose from. The first—which costs nothing—is called a **"guaranteed purchase"** option, which assures you the right to purchase additional incremental long-term care insurance coverage in the future without having to prove that you are still insurable. Instead, though, you may choose to add an **"inflation rider"** benefit to your policy, for which you'll need to pay additional premium. If you purchase the inflation rider, the Knights of Columbus automatically increases the dollar amount of your coverage by 5 percent each year on a compound basis. If you don't choose the inflation rider, you automatically are covered by the guaranteed purchase option mentioned above at no additional cost. If you choose to exercise the options later, your premium for the additional coverage will be determined by your attained age.

There are other riders and options available as well. One is the **"non-forfeiture"** rider, and another is the

"return of premium" rider. Contact your local Knights of Columbus field agent for a more detailed explanation of these as well as the other options mentioned above.

Eligibility to Receive Benefits

Here's the official statement about benefit eligibility that appears on the Knights of Columbus long-term care insurance policy.

> *"To be eligible for benefits provided by this contract, you must be certified as a chronically ill individual pursuant to a plan of care prescribed by a licensed healthcare practitioner. Benefits are payable only for qualified long-term care services, and all benefits are subject to our maximum lifetime benefit. Certain benefits are subject to your maximum monthly benefit."*[45]

A **"chronically ill individual"** is someone who is unable to perform—without substantial assistance—at least **two of the six** Activities of Daily Living for a period of time that is **expected to last at least 90 day**s or that requires **substantial supervision to protect** the individual from threats to health due to severe cognitive impairment. In Chapter 3, the Activities of Daily Living were listed and defined. They include: bathing, continence, dressing, eating, toileting and transferring. Activities of Daily Living relate to personal independence in everyday living, and **are used as a measurement standard to determine someone's ability to function independently.**

---

[45] Knights of Columbus Long-Term Care Insurance Policy.

A licensed health care professional—your physician, a registered professional nurse, or a licensed social worker, for example—can determine that you qualify to begin receiving long-term care benefits by evaluating how well you function using the Activities of Daily Living.

Evaluating Coverage and Options

Let's take a look at some options. **Facilities Only Care** coverage is less expensive than **Comprehensive Care** coverage. Remember, **Comprehensive Care** coverage provides benefits in a nursing facility, assisted living facility, or in your home.

The **number of days** for which you want coverage determines the cost of either a **Comprehensive Care** or **Facilities Only Care** policy. The riders that you choose will also affect the annual premium. In the earlier part of this chapter, I've used illustrations including **Facilities Only Care** and **Comprehensive Care** coverage costs. In order to calculate the cost of your policy with appropriate coverage, it will be necessary, given your age, to price your policy with the help of a Knights of Columbus insurance agent. He can develop the exact cost per month, quarter, semi-annually, or annually.

Here's another strategy **for you to talk about with your Knights of Columbus field agent.** You could buy companion policies: a **Comprehensive Care** policy, say, with benefits of $50 per day, and a **Facilities Only Care** policy with benefits of $100 per day. The **Comprehensive Care** policy would allow you to have care in your home and have up to $50 per day of the costs covered. If you were to move into an assisted living facility, your **Facilities Only Care** policy would pay benefits of up to $100 a day, and currently, that should pretty much cover the current daily cost of an assisted living facility.

But if at some time you needed to go to a nursing home, you could **receive benefits from both of your policies.** Together, they provide benefits of up to $150 per day and that could cover the current average daily cost of nursing home care. You could do the same if you needed more than $100 per day coverage in the assisted living facility. We are, of course, using numbers that represent the average costs in the country today. An inflation rider would help to keep that cost covered with the same combination of policies. You can manage your long-term care needs and use the policies in any sequence or combination and be covered.

Why would you have two policies? As we've just seen, having two policies provides flexibility for care and reduces costs. Since the **Facilities Only Care** policy costs less than the **Comprehensive Care** policy, a combination like this could be used to save you some premium dollars. Once you understand that long-term care is not just nursing home care, this flexibility gives you more choices to manage your care. Since 70 percent of the people responding to an informal survey expressed a preference to have their long-term care at home, at least some **Comprehensive Care** coverage would be needed.

This two-policy approach provides the most flexibility to fund and use long-term care. The inflation rider can be included or left off. The option for adding inflationary increases is flexible between the two policies, so even the inflation protection can be monitored and increased in real time. This allows you to base each of your inflation protection decisions on your health history, your attained age, income level, and actual marketplace cost increases for care and to make changes in your coverage every two years. If you don't exactly understand all of this, don't worry right now. Contact your local Knights of Columbus agent for a thorough explanation.

As you consider a long-term care insurance policy, you should <u>purchase the broadest coverage your budget will reasonably allow</u>, so that your care options are not too limited. At the very least, you should have **"Facilities Only Care"** coverage.

If You're Not Eligible for a Knights of Columbus Policy...

You cannot buy a Knights of Columbus long-term care insurance policy unless you are a member or the spouse of a member. Also, you may be uninsurable because of health reasons.

However, if even one of you is insurable, there is help available for you and your family. All Knights of Columbus long-term care policyholders <u>and their family members</u> have access to a national network of <u>long-term care providers</u> who have agreed to discount their rates and fees from 7.5 to 22.5 percent below retail. The Knights of Columbus is partnering with LifePlans, Inc. to provide member families with one-stop shopping for a full spectrum of long-term care services at discounted rates. Just by having a policy in place, you become eligible to use these services. Take a look at the following discounts that have been negotiated for you:

- Home Health Services (average discount: 13 percent)
- Durable Medical Equipment (average discount: 22.5 percent)
- Adult Daycare (average discount: 9 percent)
- Assisted Living Facilities (average discount: 10 percent)
- Skilled Nursing Facilities (average discount: 7.5 percent)
- Hospice Care (average discount: 15 percent)

There are over 9,000 provider service options available. Services are available in all 50 states and the District of Columbia. One important component of a comprehensive home health care program that is covered is a Personal Emergency Response System or PERS. A PERS in your home provides an immediate response in an emergency using a "Help Button" that activates a signal to the Response Center. Another service included is Hearing Aids. All of the contracted providers meet established state and federal credentialing requirements.

Using LifePlans Provider Pathway Program for the Services You Need

Here's how the plan works. You contact LifePlans. They will provide you with a list of long-term care services in your area and coordinate the service you need. You can select the service from the list, or you may identify a potential provider not yet in the LifePlans network that could be added through you as an individual or as a provider for everyone.

Once you choose a provider, all bills for care and services are sent by the provider directly to LifePlans. LifePlans re-prices the bills using the contracted discount rate, and then sends the new discounted bill to either the long-term care policyholder or the family member for payment. Payment is due within 30 days of billing.

This plan can provide a very impressive savings. Here's a real-life example. The caregiver sent a bill for $5,500 to LifePlans, and the bill was re-written to a new amount of $ 4,675.00. This family saved $825 every month that they would have had to pay from their own pockets—and the quality of care received was exactly the same.

In 2004, the average person using the LifePlans Provider Pathway saved almost $300 per month. Of course if you receive very little care, your savings will be much less. If you receive many hours of home health care or facility care, savings can be as high as $800 per month or more!

A person doesn't have to be on a long-term care claim to be eligible for the discounts for the Provider Pathway service providers. Costs associated with care during the elimination period can also be discounted. The program saves benefit dollars, thereby stretching policy benefits for insureds.

An important advantage of using LifePlans is that it checks the accuracy of the bills it receives from your health care service providers before the bills are re-priced and sent on to you, your long-term care insurer, or a family member. This can be especially significant if you are not totally familiar with the bills, or billing methods, or if you don't have the capacity to review and check them yourself.

You say, "Well, what will that cost me?" There is no cost! All start-up costs have been paid for by the Knights of Columbus.

So if **you** have a long-term care policy from the Knights of Columbus and if **your spouse, parents, parents-in-law, or dependent children need care,** they will be able to access these long-term care services at a discount. For more information and details, contact your local Knights of Columbus insurance agent.

Your Knights of Columbus Long-Term Care Policy Does More!

With this added benefit of discounted long-term care services, owning a Knights of Columbus long-term care policy extends your reach. For example, assume that the chances of a person needing long-term care is as low as one in three. Let's say that you and your spouse each have living parents. Of the six of you, two are likely to need long-term care, although in reality, it's more likely that three of the six will need some long-term care in their lifetime. So even if only you have a very basic long-term care insurance policy from the Knights of Columbus, any of the six of you will be able to take advantage of these services and discounts. Therefore, it is most likely that if you have coverage, someone in your family will have access to discounted benefits they need.

People who are financially successful don't necessarily make the right decision every time, but they don't make big mistakes, either. They most likely would not make a mistake that would leave any of their assets vulnerable to be lost or stolen or spent unnecessarily. They use insurance to minimize the risks—to protect their assets. Do you have other types of insurance to minimize your own financial risks? Then why is long-term care insurance the one insurance that you don't yet own?

No one knows what long-term care will be like in 10 or 20 years. So should you wait until the last minute until you make plans to pay for your long-term care? It is highly unlikely that the government is going to put in place a comprehensive new program that will pay for all of the long-term care that you and all of the aging baby boomers will need in a few years. In fact, the health care system is extremely vulnerable right now. As pressure grows to ease the financial burden on social security, pressure will also grow to eliminate the elderly and infirm to "free-up" more money for the "fit" and those who contribute more than they take from society. What will that mean for you?

Tax Incentives

Minnesota currently gives a $100 state tax credit to people who own an appropriately sized long-term care insurance policy. Some other states are offering similar incentives. Some states even have a provision to provide shelter for assets if they have long-term care coverage. Check with your local Knights of Columbus insurance agent for information about incentives provided by your state.

Since January 1977, individuals have been able to include out-of-pocket expenses for long-term care and <u>long-term care insurance premiums</u> with their other itemized medical expenses on their annual federal tax returns. To the extent that they exceed the federal government's 7.5 percent threshold of adjusted gross income, these expenses are deductible as long as you have a tax-qualified policy. Knights of Columbus policies are tax qualified. On the other hand, benefits from long-term care insurance are tax-free as long as they do not exceed the actual cost of care. If they do exceed the actual cost of care, the extra amount would be taxable.

And since January 1997, when an insurance company pays benefits for long-term care, the company must report it to the IRS using Form 1099-LTC. If you have questions regarding taxes and long-term care, consult your tax advisor or accountant for details on your specific situation.

Something for Everyone

The Knights of Columbus long-term care insurance offers multiple options, from plans that cover only nursing home or assisted living costs to plans that are all-encompassing and cover at-home care costs. You have options to select the amount and length of coverage, and better still, if you're married, your premium is discounted, and if you and your spouse are both approved, the discount is even greater. An option to using the discount is to use the "shared care" option and use each others' benefits.

So there's no doubt that you will be able to custom-fit a long-term care insurance policy—or policies for you and your spouse—to fulfill your own needs, goals, and budget. You will be safeguarding your assets and assuring that you'll have all of the long-term care you need whenever you need it.

Knights of Columbus Insurance: There When You Need It

In 1882, Father Michael J. McGivney envisioned an organization to help Catholic families devastated by the death of the family breadwinner. From those humble beginnings, the Knights of Columbus has grown to be the largest Catholic family fraternal organization in the world.

Today, Knights of Columbus Insurance continues Father McGivney's vision to care for members and their families' financial wellbeing. **Knights of Columbus Insurance is among the strongest insurance companies in North America:**

- Ranks in the top 5 percent of approximately 2,000 insurance companies throughout North America[46]
- Received the highest possible ratings from A.M. Best (A++ Superior) and Standard & Poor's (AAA Extremely Strong)

---

[46] Based on total value of assets, as published in The National Underwriter.

- A member of the Insurance Marketplace Standards Association (IMSA), reserved only for those insurance companies that conduct their business by the highest ethical standards.

But there's even more to Knights of Columbus than its financial strength and stability. As an organization, the Knights of Columbus helps support a multitude of charitable causes. This means that the Knights of Columbus not only make a difference in your life, but a difference in the lives of countless others.

Your Knights of Columbus insurance agent is more than a brother Knight. He is a dedicated, knowledgeable, and experienced professional, qualified to design comprehensive solutions to your financial needs that fit your goals, your lifestyle, and your budget. Additionally, he can help you learn more about Knights of Columbus retirement annuities and life insurance plans that can provide you with well-rounded financial protection. If you need the name of an agent in your area, call 1-800-345-5632.

Asking the Right Questions

This book cannot possibly give you all the answers—it was never intended to do that. But it <u>will</u> set you on a path to learning about aging, long-term care, and long-term care insurance. If you use the material in this book, you'll know what questions to ask—and who to ask—to discover what options are available to you. It will help you narrow your focus so you can make the best decisions and plans for yourself.

If you want to learn more, seek advice on your specific situation from your Knights of Columbus insurance agent and any other qualified professional you need to consult. They can put together a plan so you will be able to access long-term care coverage when you need it.

May God bless you and keep you healthy so you never need long-term care. And, if you do, may He grant you the wisdom and foresight to plan for it now.

APPENDIX

The author and publisher of this book provide the following sources and contact information only for the convenience of the reader. It is not meant to imply an endorsement or recommendation of any of them.

Books

A Shopper's Guide to Long-Term Care Insurance by The National Association of Insurance Commissioners
Alzheimer's Disease: the Family Journey Caron, Pattee and Otteson, North Ridge Press, 2000
Caregiving and Personal Assistants—How to Find, Hire and Manage the People Who Help You (or Your Loved One) DeGraff, A., Saratoga Access Publications, Inc., 2002
Nursing Homes and Assisted Living Facilities: Your Practical Guide for Making the Right Decision Connell, L., Sphinx Publishing 2003
The Complete Idiot's Guide to Long-Term Care Planning Driscoll, M., Marie Butler-Knight, 2003
There's No Place Like a Nursing Home Shoff, K., published by Invisible Ink Press, 2002

Don Kramer
E-mail: kramerdon@aol.com
Web Site: donkramer.com

BIOGRAPHY

In 2003, Don Kramer sold more long-term care policies for the Knights of Columbus than any of their agents in America. He is a member of the prestigious Million Dollar Round Table and the National Association of Insurance and Financial Advisors. He has earned the Fraternal Insurance Counsellor (FIC) designation. Don regularly conducts seminars on long-term care and related issues.

Don was elected to the Minnesota State Senate where he served on committees dealing with Health Care and Family Services. He was named Legislator of the Year in his first year by Arc Minnesota. These experiences, and having had his mother, father-in-law, mother-in-law, and brother in home care, assisted living and long-term care facilities, has given him knowledge and skills he uses to help the people he serves.

Don is well respected for services to the members in all his assigned councils. The Minnesota Knights of Columbus Council has recognized him with the Directors Award three years in a row and in 2004 named him top insurance agent in the state. He has qualified for incentive awards every year he has been a field agent. Last year he qualified for the Supreme Knights Club. Don uses his experience and training to understand the needs of people just like you. As a Brother Knight, he has a special perspective on your situation.

"We're so sorry Grandma, but..."